HEMISFAIR '68

AND THE TRANSFORMATION OF SAN ANTONIO

San Antonio, Apr. 6-Oct. 6.— Void if detached — Admit One
Texas World's Fair
HemisFair '68® $2⁰⁰ U.S.
00326
No es válido si se desprende del talonario—Una Entrada

HemisFair '68
and the Transformation
of San Antonio

Sterlin Holmesly

MAVERICK PUBLISHING COMPANY

MAVERICK PUBLISHING COMPANY
P.O. Box 6355, San Antonio, Texas 78209

Library of Congress Cataloging-in-Publication Data

Holmesly, Sterlin, 1932-
  HemisFair '68 and the transformation of San Antonio / Sterlin
Holmesly.
    p. cm.
  ISBN 1-893271-28-5
  1. HemisFair (1968 : San Antonio, Tex.) 2. San Antonio
(Tex.)--History. I. Title.
  T8711968 .B2 H65
  976.4'351--dc21
                                                2003003629

Printed in the United States of America on acid-free paper

Frontispiece: H. B. Zachry Co. cranes lift fully furnished modular rooms into
place to complete the Hilton Palacio del Rio Hotel in 202 days, in time for
the opening of HemisFair. The Hilton, San Antonio's first major new
hotel since pre-Depression days, became the first in a series of major hotels
as the city's HemisFair-inspired convention industry rapidly expanded.
ZINTGRAFF COLLECTION, UNIVERSITY OF TEXAS INSTITUTE OF TEXAN CULTURES AT SAN ANTONIO

Contents

Preface

HemisFair '68 proved to be a watershed event for San Antonio, one that united and changed the city. Its legacy is still changing the city. This book contains some key accounts of HemisFair and its aftermath.

Without HemisFair, San Antonio would not have had the Convention Center and the burgeoning convention and visitors industry. The resulting new hotels and intense River Walk development serve some seven million visitors annually in a $3 billion annual industry. Since the military's shrinking with closure of Kelly Air Force Base, that industry has become the city's largest.

Without the HemisFair Arena there would probably have been no San Antonio Spurs basketball team. The Texas Pavilion–turned–Institute of Texan Cultures, and its rich resources, would not exist.

Since HemisFair, other changes have rolled through San Antonio—in social relations, in politics, in economic development. Many of those stories are also recounted.

No story of the HemisFair year would be complete without treating another 1968 watershed event, one that created what became the University of Texas Health Science Center at San Antonio. A crucial Commissioners Court vote that year created a tax to finish building a Bexar County teaching hospital, without which there could have been no medical school. A complex of private medical and research facilities now surrounds the Health Science Center, providing thousands of well-paying jobs. The story of that vote and its results are included.

These accounts are edited oral history interviews inspired, inadvertently, by Brig. Gen. Robert McDermott (USAF ret.). In the early 1990s, I listened to him tell of coming to San Antonio during the World's Fair and of his efforts to spur economic development. "Someone ought to get this down," I said to myself.

Since I had been in San Antonio before, during and long after HemisFair, I took on the project and conducted the interviews sporadically, mainly in the mid-1990s. It was planned as a representative cross-section of voices rather than as an encyclopedic one, and I regret that limitations of time and resources prevented including more. Some of the interviewees—Tom Berg, Henry Guerra and Blair Reeves—are no longer living. I thank all of those who agreed to be interviewed and tell their stories.

I turned to the Institute of Texas Cultures for support and received enthusiastic help in many areas. Dr. Rex Ball, the executive director, and his staff have provided audiotapes, transcriptions, photographs and computer disks. Laurie Gudzikowski of the Programs Division has been exceptionally helpful, as has Librarian Kendra Trachta. Tom Shelton helped with the photos. The entire collection of unedited transcipts is housed at the institute, as is an oral history of jazz that I did in the early 1980s.

I would also like to thank *Express-News* Publisher Larry Walker for suggesting that excerpts of some interviews run in the newspaper's Insight section, as they did. I am grateful to Linda Vaughn, who did a superb job of editing and displaying those interviews. I thank Lynell J. Burkett of the *Express-News* for conducting the interviews of Ernie Cortes and Helen Ayala. Editor Robert Rivard opened the paper's photo files for this book, and Assistant Managing Editor Kathy Foley and Librarian Kelly Guckian dug through the archives to find the right pictures.

Also, a thank you to Lewis Fisher of Maverick Publishing Company for recognizing a book where others couldn't.

Finally, this one's for my wife, Sydney, who saw that there was a book before anyone else, including me.

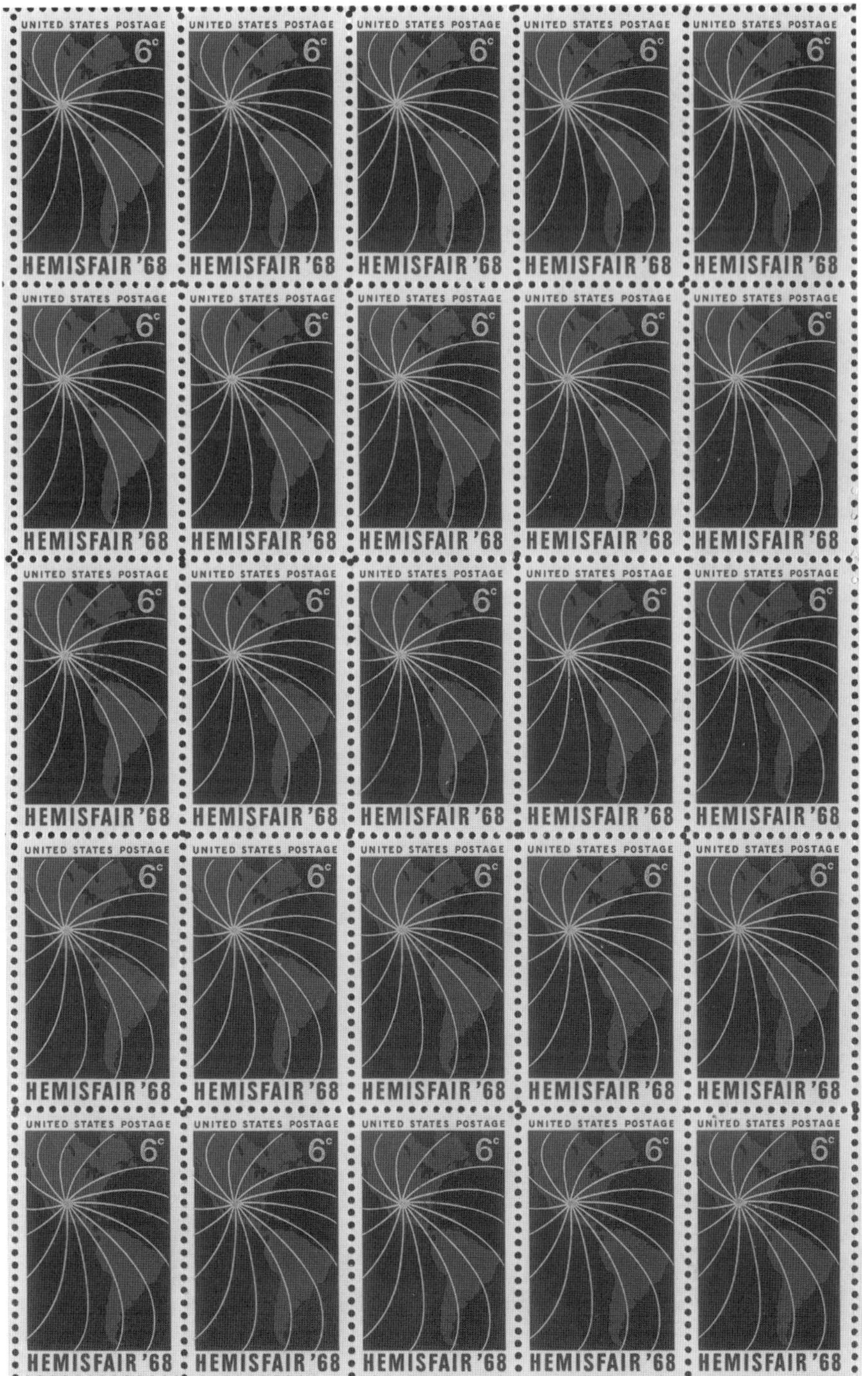
UNITED STATES POSTAGE
6c
HEMISFAIR '68

TOP: ZINTGRAFF COLLECTION, UT INSTITUTE OF TEXAN CULTURES
BELOW: *EXPRESS-NEWS* COLLECTION, UT INSTITUTE OF TEXAN CULTURES

1. HemisFair '68

San Antonio's economy had been stagnant since it lost the position as the largest city in Texas to Dallas in the census of 1930. Three decades later, a group of businessmen determined to wrest San Antonio out of its lethargy by putting on a world's fair to celebrate the 250th anniversary of the city's founding in 1718.

Several sites were considered. The one chosen was in the heart of downtown, in a somewhat rundown neighborhood not far from the languishing River Walk. There the city qualified for federal urban renewal funds for construction of an exhibit hall–arena–theater complex. Restoration of two dozen historic homes on the grounds highlighted the city's picturesque character, as did extension of the River Walk into the grounds. Having sufficient corporate participation to qualify as a World's Fair was aided by having a Texan in the White House.

With the name HemisFair invented to reflect the theme "The Confluence of Civilizations in the Americas," the fair opened on April 6, 1968 for a five-month run. After closing, the exhibit hall–arena–theater became a convention center that catapulted the visitor industry into, ultimately, the city's largest. The United States Pavilion became a Federal Courthouse complex. The Texas Pavilion became the Institute of Texan Cultures. And the Tower of the Americas became the symbol of the modern city of San Antonio.

These three accounts reflect the anguish of planning and the ingenuity which created this transforming event.

William R. Sinkin: *Organizing HemisFair*

Then president of Texas State Bank, Bill Sinkin served as the first president of HemisFair '68.

My strong feeling was, and still is, that HemisFair was a watershed for San Antonio's growth and development. The concept was to give San An-

---

Facing page: The residential neighborhood in foreground of the 1957 view at top was transformed 11 years later into the grounds of HemisFair, including the signature Tower of the Americas, a domed arena-theater-convention center complex and, at lower left, the two buildings of the United States Pavilion, a federal courthouse complex after the fair.

tonio a place in the sun and to bring the community together as a cohesive force. It did both in a remarkable fashion.

Until HemisFair we were a good city, a quiet city, with not much vision or thrust for the future. And I really think the dynamic change began with the election for the first time of a Hispanic to the Congress of the United States, Henry B. Gonzalez. He went to Congress with his 20th Century plan for the 20th district. HemisFair was the number one issue, A Fair of the Americas: a fair for trade and tourism that would help San Antonio grow and develop.

I am happy to say I was engaged in every campaign he was in. Congressman Gonzalez had a vision. Time proved him to be absolutely correct. Hemis-Fair brought to San Antonio an eclectic group

After signing the HemisFair bill into law on Oct. 25, 1965, President Lyndon B. Johnson presents Congressman Henry B. Gonzalez with the pen he used.

of citizens. It brought artists. It brought designers. It brought thinkers. It brought excitement and group dynamics in developing ideas for a fair. It was a cohesive force. I can never remember in the history of San Antonio where a bond issue, for instance, passed in every single precinct of the community, as our $30 million bond issue for HemisFair did, under the leadership of Walter McAllister. And of Henry B.

We began to get a profile in the United States and in Latin America. We became more important to Mexico, and they became determined to open up one of the most significant of the pavilions there. Other countries looked and said, "Well, San Antonio has so much to offer, it's been an undiscovered place to visit." With that came creation for HemisFair of the extension of the river, now a masterpiece of showmanship for San Antonio tourism.

Two things happened to San Antonio after the fair. One, the dynamism and activity and thrust that made the fair possible sort of played out. Everybody was pretty tired. We'd just gone through a magnificent program with nearly five million visitors, we had gotten our place in the sun, and we were ready for something else. We weren't sure what.

But coalitions that grew up and contacts and network developed during HemisFair began to make a contribution. The additional tourism, because now we had a convention center, was a real contribution. We had some more hotel rooms. We had some more people here who were artists, designers, graphic people, writers, and there was a bubbling up of a lot of activity that San Antonio had never experienced. So San Antonio was never the same after HemisFair, though it took a while for it to begin to grow.

Even though HemisFair lost money itself, the city didn't lose a dime. The whole thing was paid for by the business community. We had permanent buildings, thanks to the insistence of our congressman that if he got money the buildings would have to remain. We had a good review of the fair in the country and overseas. No untoward incidents occurred. So it was a happy time for the greatest coming together San Antonio has ever had.

That was an inheritance that we, of the 1970s and '80s and '90s, have been able to use. The development of San Antonio had begun to change, in terms of growth becoming absolutely paramount. Our sensitivity to one of the key problems of the community, our reliance for water on the Edwards Aquifer, had not yet been developed, but that began in the '70s.

But the community had learned that there were other segments of the community, and we empowered them. They could contribute to the success of a community. One was labor. We brought labor in. Hispanics certainly began to be involved. For the first time we had some good African American leadership, who felt that the fair was for them as well. And if you looked at the mix of people who came to the fair, you knew that HemisFair was a statement for San Antonio as a community, rather than for a group of people or people who could afford to go to something others couldn't.

There were race riots elsewhere at the time that some thought could spread here and hurt the fair. But San Antonio has never had a race riot. I have a theory for this that goes back to the Good Government League beginning a process of opening doors. They began to support or select, say, a Hispanic for an office. That opening of a window or door, really instituted by Bob Sawtelle, a guru of what community politics ought to be, left a feeling that there was a place for Mexican Americans in the community. Plus the leadership of Episcopal Bishop Everett Jones, Catholic Archbishop Robert Lucey and Rabbi David Jacobson in implementing peaceful lunch counter integration meant there was already a sensitivity in this community, and there wasn't a harshness that really bred race riots.

Also, we didn't have race riots because of HemisFair. We said that we can't have a World's Fair and be a host to the world if we have segregated operations—if they can't go in and get a drink, if we can't be civilized and be able to offer mixed drinks and have our visitors, from wherever they are, go into a restaurant.

So in 1962 after Henry B. Gonzalez went up to Congress, he called me one Saturday morning when I had the store at Centeno's on West Commerce Street and said, "I want to have a Fair of the Americas and I'd like for you to call a group together and talk about it."

And I said, "Well, Henry, what are we doing up there?"

He said, "That's going to be the job of the community, but I want to do something and develop trade and develop commerce and develop our presence in Mexico and Central America."

So I called a meeting of some 35 people that February at the Plaza Hotel—and, by the way, we all paid for our own lunch. Morris Jaffe was there, Tom Frost, Forrest Smith, H. B. Zachry. We had a good group. And we talked about the fair. And we had almost every banker there, by the way. The response was good.

But they said, "How do we know the community will buy this? What are we going to tell the community we're going to do? What is a fair? What are we talking about?"

Well, we got a name during that discussion that came up. Some people say Jerry Harris was the one who initiated the name HemisFair. And I spent a year, I guess, going around the community, going to Seguin, as well as to Luling and all the communities around here, talking about a fair. I made some 200 speeches that year, I guess, to anybody who would listen. We'd go to the dairies and they'd crown a little cow Miss HemisFair.

In 1963, after we felt that something could be done, we went to the bankers; I was in banking at that time. We asked the local bankers' organization for a loan, $7,500, to hire Economic Research Associates to make a study. They made the study. We had a community dinner and they said, "If you spent $8 million, and if you spent $100 million on this, so much on this, you'd get six million visitors and could have a fair."

William R. Sinkin, HemisFair's first president, right, with Mayor Walter B. McAllister.

We took that report and organized. I became president of the fair, Zachry became chairman of the board. I think Marshall Steves at that time became involved, after the first year became vice president, because he succeeded me. The three of us and John Daniels, the attorney, incorporated San Antonio Fair Inc. in 1963, and that was the beginning.

It was then up to us to raise $7.5 million to pay for operation of this fair. So Marshall went out raising funds with the help of Tom Frost and some other bankers, but used his very aggressive and dynamite approach. In record time we had $7.5 million underwritten to hire people to run the fair, promote it and develop it, bring people in and develop our logo, everything.

The $30 million bond issue came in 1964, and then we had to get money from the federal government, the state government and then sign up participants.

Fortunately, we had a strong friend in Gov. John Connally. And he was a key player in us getting the Institute of Texan Cultures. Henry B. was committed to getting us federal funding. And the city was committed, be-

HemisFair Arena's framework rises in the background as two of the old neighborhood's homes await restoration. The 1840s home at left became India's pavilion.

cause at the beginning when we decided to go for the fair I went to Walter McAllister, who was mayor.

I said, "Mayor, I know that you and Henry are at polarized lengths in politics, but, for the community, if you and Henry would be honorary co-chairs—you're the most powerful political figure, he's the most powerful congressman—we'll do the work, but we need your commitment to make it work."

Well, if you remember Mr. McAllister you know he was a pretty strong conservative, but he was a gentleman. He sort of looked at me and started to smile. He said, "Bill, if Henry will do it, I'll do it. I believe this will work."

Well, we put it together. We appointed a committee of 21, which met every Tuesday morning at 7:30 for four and a half years. We never had less than 18 people there. A totally devoted committee. And that's why the bond of $30 million passed. That's why the elements of leadership stayed involved. And that's why the media, which became our blessing, just took care of us. We couldn't do anything wrong.

I was very close to Senator Ralph Yarborough. There were others on the executive committee who just didn't like him, and we had some problems—one time Ralph threatened to kill the HemisFair bill—because they just didn't pay any attention to him for a while, not recognizing that you just don't go around a senator.

Yarborough and President Lyndon Johnson had a truce about what was going to happen. Lyndon wanted this fair for Henry B., because he told Henry, "I'm going to get you that money." And I remember going up with Henry B. and John Daniels and Claude Pepper, who was on the committee that voted the money, and going to Lyndon, and he said, "Well, Henry, here's what I told you I was going to do."

We went up and testified before the Senate and the House. But Yarborough did carry the bill.

But I do want to tell you, there were some hard feelings in the beginning. But it was ameliorated. The fair sort of became a glue that brought people together. It got exciting that this was going to happen. This World's Fair is here and all these people coming in. Six million visitors, and it's going to be glamorous and happy and it's going to be the biggest fiesta we ever had. So it brought us together.

The fair lost money, but I think it was like $16.8 million. The underwriters went through three underwritings. We started out with four and a half, and then six, five, I think, five and a half, and then seven, and seven and a half million. We had to go three times to the trough because things were costing more.

The perfect HemisFair story is the story of this small place off Alamo Plaza that was almost like a little gazebo, selling fried chicken. I had to go to this man and tell him that we were taking this with urban renewal, because this is where the fair was going. And he started to cry. He said, "You're putting me out of business." We said, "We'll find you another location, we'll try, we don't want to be cruel." We moved him. And the result was Church's Fried Chicken.

On balance, you know, I think we had HemisFair at a time when San Antonio was ready for something. We were still bemoaning that we'd lost the State Fair to Dallas in 1936. And in 1958 we were still crying about it, you see. This just changed our inferiority complex.

HemisFair, I want to reiterate, was a watershed of economics and tourism growth for San Antonio. It's a permanent legacy that will be hard to match, because for the first time there was a confluence not only of civilizations, which was our theme, but there was a true confluence in the community. There was a very, very minimum of disgruntlement or criticism of HemisFair. It was truly a cooperative symphony of harmony for San Antonio.

A 20-minute ride on the Mini-Monorail, facing page, gave some a leisurely overview of HemisFair's 92 acres, while others took a cruise on the lagoon. Germany's pavilion, above, featured a geographical presentation of the then-divided nation and its old capital, Berlin, accessed in those Cold War days by only the three air corridors highlighted in lights. The onetime Solomon Halff house lawn, right, became the Cafe de Paris, the indoors a French restaurant.
Following page: *Four of Mexico's Los Volodores Flying Indians fanned out down a 114-foot pole, in an ancient Aztec spectacle sponsored by Frito-Lay/ Pepsi-Cola.*

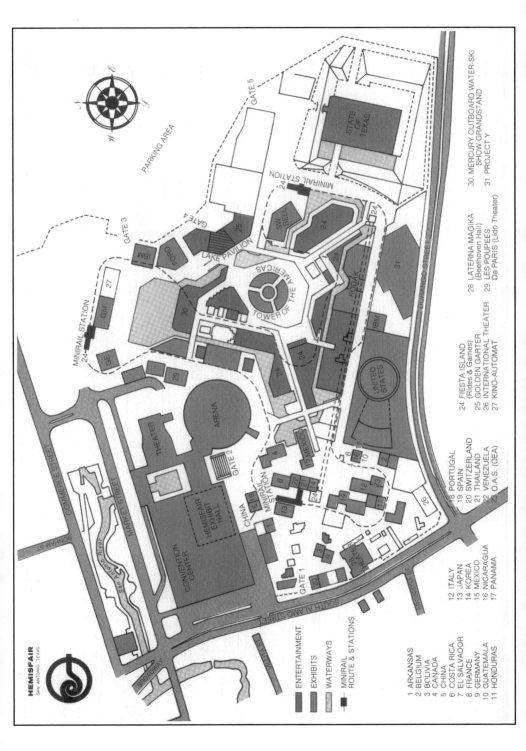

HEMISFAIR
SAN ANTONIO, TEXAS

ENTERTAINMENT
EXHIBITS
WATERWAYS
MINIRAIL
ROUTE & STATIONS

1 ARKANSAS
2 BELGIUM
3 BOLIVIA
4 CANADA
5 CHINA
6 COSTA RICA
7 EL SALVADOR
8 FRANCE
9 GERMANY
10 GUATEMALA
11 HONDURAS

12 ITALY
13 JAPAN
14 KOREA
15 MEXICO
16 NICARAGUA
17 PANAMA

18 PORTUGAL
19 SPAIN
20 SWITZERLAND
21 THAILAND
22 VENEZUELA
23 O.A.S. (OEA)

24 FIESTA ISLAND
   (Rides & Games)
25 GOLDEN GARTER
26 INTERNATIONAL THEATER
27 KINO-AUTOMAT

28 LATERNA MAGIKA
   (Beethoven Hall)
29 LES POUPEES
   De PARIS (Lido Theater)

30 MERCURY OUTBOARD WATER-SKI
   SHOW GRANDSTAND
31 PROJECT Y

RJR FOODS

Boone Powell: *Building the Tower of the Americas*

Boone Powell, project architect for HemisFair '68's signature Tower of the Americas, is a principal in the architectural firm of Ford, Powell & Carson. He worked briefly for its founder, O'Neil Ford, in 1956 and 1958 and rejoined the firm in 1960, becoming a partner some six years later.

The Tower of the Americas literally was the theme structure of HemisFair. Within the fair's executive committee there was some discussion about the kind of theme structure to have. Pat Zachry had a number of ideas, even one of having a great statue of Lyndon Johnson and Mexican President Diaz Ordaz "caught in the act of *abrazo*," as he described it.

This was just one of many issues about the tower and its design. Another was about how tall it was to be. When construction began, the city hadn't yet funded the mast on the top, which, as towers go, is always counted as part of the height of the tower. But the mast had not been authorized, so some press releases went out stating that it was 622 feet high.

Soon after the tower started, the city executed the contract to go ahead and complete the mast on top, so it became 750 feet, and as such it probably was the tallest observation tower in the Western Hemisphere at that time. It was obviously not nearly as tall as the Empire State Building or some other commercial buildings. I think the tower that first eclipsed it was in Toronto.

Construction on the tower began in February 1967. It was completed right at the time the fair opened. I heard recently that the fair was ready to open but was delayed a day or two, because of the Martin Luther King assassination and a concern that some kind of event might ripple from that situation. I had previously thought the reason it opened late was just because of construction.

How did we build the tower? Well, we had very good foundation material about 50 feet under the tower. The first thing we did was drill 36-inch piers, 55 of them. They went down and belled out into blue shale around 60 feet below ground level. Then we poured the piers, starting about 15 to 16 feet below grade and going down from there.

At that point, still below grade, a great pier cap was poured to unify all 55 piers. The pier cap was about eight feet thick, of solid concrete and almost 100 feet in diameter. Then the lower part of the shaft was poured up to the top of the buttresses. That section went up from the pier cap to around

22 feet above grade. At that point, the shaft shape we recognize as the tower commences in earnest, and goes all the way up to the tophouse.

That material was all reinforced concrete, being slip-formed at a certain rate each day. It changed as it went up, in terms of the concrete reinforcement in the lower level. At 200 and at 400 feet the design changed internally; externally it looks the same. At about 540 feet it changed again, because now we're inside where the tophouse will be. So the interior of the shaft became stairs and small rooms.

Above about 590 feet it becomes much more solid. Embedments are placed at that point, 12 above and 12 below, to bring in the 12 major trusses and weld them back into the core. The tophouse hangs from those trusses. On top is the elevator penthouse; above that the mast. The structure was all completed in about 14 months despite some difficulties encountered during the tophouse lift.

Tower of the Americas project architect Boone Powell.

We developed the intricate 12-pointed shape of the shaft early on, and that in turn helped generate three different designs that were ultimately scaled down to make the final design more realistic in terms of the crowds that would be at HemisFair and of the amount of space that could be afforded. The final design at 750 feet is the one we built.

As we were working on this process, the money to develop those plans was coming from the HemisFair Corporation, which had limited funding and was spreading it around to lots of different things. To develop the basic design we had been paid only about 20 percent of the total fee that would ultimately be needed. Normally you spend about 75 percent of the fee on plans before you start building a building like this. The key thing about that is that with only $64,000 we were strapped just to get drawings made. With little resources, and lacking basic testing information, our structural engineer, Ray Pinnell, was having a hard time and couldn't really design the steel that was needed.

We did know one thing: we had a special problem. Ray and I began talking one day about a great concern he had: What was the overturning moment? What's the coefficient of drag of the tower shaft shape in the wind? That was a serious question, because it could vary a lot. If it was twice as much as he assumed, it would mean we would need twice or more the amount of steel, a huge factor. So Ray came up with an idea. Since we had no money for a wind tunnel test, we'd get the two leading experts in fluid mechanics in the state—one at Texas A&M and the other at the Unviersity of Texas—to give opinions of what it would be.

To give you some point of reference, a square shape with winds passing across it has a coefficient of drag of 1.0. So that sets the base everything is related to. A cylinder the same size across has a coefficient of drag of .33, just one-third as much. And a sheet of paper, or sheet-like form, with wind going around it has a coefficient of drag of 2.0. It's all very neat, precise. This is the way these shapes test out in a wind tunnel.

So Ray wrote them both and got answers back. I think the professor at UT thought that because of all the angulations of the shape of the tower—the 12 points and the spaces in between it—it would perform like a sheet of paper and have a coefficient of drag of 2.0. That would mean the tower would have to be extraordinarily stout and would need so much steel that there would be a serious problem of cost. The professor at A&M said he thought the wind would read this as a cylinder and the coefficient of drag would be .33, one-sixth as much.

As we struggled with that and thought further of developing the tower and the tophouse, and the various design aspects of it, at first we didn't know what to do.

We sat down one day, and Ray said maybe we could make a simple test, because water and air behave the same. He said, "Could we find a place where there's any moving water?" And I said, "Well, we could go out south on the San Antonio River just below Espada Dam, and there's a little area I know there where there's a good bit of water flow." He said, "Well, we need to do something, because we can't go on, since we have this opinion from UT."

So we got Marshall Steves to make us a square shape about two feet long, and we got one like the shape of the Tower of the America's shaft, as

In the absence of funds for a wind tunnel, structural engineer Ray Pinnell, left, tests the future tower's coefficient of drag in the current of the San Antonio River with Ford, Powell & Carson's Milton Babbitt.

well as a cylinder made the same length and the same size across. We screwed eyehooks into the ends and got some weights to hold the shapes down in the river. We made a bridle to hold the shape down in the water, then another bridle hooked up to a fish scale, just a simple old fish scale.

The water was running fast enough so we actually got significantly different readings. Whether they were the right readings in terms of pounds didn't matter; what we wanted was the comparison. The water sweeping across the shape of the Tower of the Americas responded approximately as it did to the cylinder, much less than it did to the square. So in a sense the square weighed three times as much as the cylinder and the shape of the Tower of the Americas. The pictures I got of this show people wading around, holding fish scales and stuff, looking like this was really an interesting game. But it wasn't just a game; it was very serious.

At that point, we felt confident that the person at A&M was right, but knew that at some point we would have to catch up and do the theoretical testing.

Finally, and after the city took over from the HemisFair Corporation, signed appropriate contracts were executed with the contractors and the design team. This was when construction began. We were able to afford wind tunnel tests. They validated the water tests we made, and validated the approach that we had taken and assumed was right. At that point, Ray Pinnell had the data to complete his structural work.

Now what's laced into this very complex issue is the fact that when they were finally ready to construct the building, and it started February 10, 1967, there was a threat of a taxpayer suit from a woman out in south San Antonio. But she had not filed a suit. I don't know if it was City Attorney Crawford Reeder or somebody else, but the city was pretty clever about this and realized she would not formally file a suit if construction were under way, because then she'd have to post a bond based on the value of the tower.

Although A. J. Lott in Houston had teamed up with Gerald Lyda, a local builder, to bid on building the tower, no contract had been signed. But without any fanfare, and in complete secrecy, a contract was signed and ground was broken in the middle of the night so the woman wouldn't file her suit. I didn't even know that ground had been broken. I simply awoke the next day, came to the office and found that the tower was under construction. That was a great shock. We still had not been advanced any more money, and plans were only 20 to 25 percent complete. Here was a 750-foot building under construction with plans little more than schematic.

Compicating this further was the fact that Mayor Walter McAllister really didn't want O'Neil Ford's firm to do the job. He didn't really like O'Neil; neither trusted the other. So we didn't get the contract for 15 to 20 days after that. We could do nothing. As I understand it, the mayor went to the city attorney and said he wanted to use somebody else. I understand the city attorney said, "It won't work. They're the ones drawing these plans, you know. No other person can assume those plans, and so legally you can't do that." Sort of hesitantly, I guess, the mayor told Public Works to go ahead and sign the contract without a switch.

But we were always playing catch-up, which is very, very scary on a project of this size. Ray hadn't even sized the steel in the basic shaft or even some of the steel in the pier caps at that point. We had an enormous amount of work to do and very little time to do it. As a consequence, we're doing working drawings trying to bring this building up to the point it should be. Gerald Lyda and A. J. Lott are out there building this sucker, I'm the project architect and every day a lot of things come up that make me feel like, if I don't get this done today, we're in trouble.

Every night the same thing. I'd lie in bed and try to go to sleep, and I would, maybe, and then I'd wake up and start thinking of one thing after another that just absolutely had to be done first thing the next morning. Had to call the superintendent, had to call this person, had to get ready to do something. I finally found that the only way I could function was to have a yellow pad there. When I'd have five or six ideas and knew I had to do them, I'd turn the light on and write them down and then go back to sleep. That was the only way it worked. I did this for about ten months. We had other major, major problems, but certainly that whole sequence of not having plans and not getting a contract until after the building was under construction for the city was one of the most difficult things I've ever done.

One of the most interesting aspects of the tower construction has to do with construction of the tower's concrete shaft. It was accomplished by a slip forming process. The slip-form developed had stainless steel surfaces, was five feet deep and was assembled directly on top of the giant pier cap. We slipped ten feet and eight inches each day as we were slipping it up.

The top surface of the pier cap is 92 feet in diameter and eight feet thick. It was level on its top surface. Then the slip-form sat on top of that and was assembled. In the beginning we were going to be pouring buttresses as well as the shaft, so the 12 ends of the basic shaft were left open, and ordinary forms were built on the outside up to 22 feet. They would slip against the slip-form so we could pour both sections together, just a normal kind of pour on part of the work, yet pour within a slipping-form on the other part, all monolithically. The buttresses that slope in toward the shaft were formed through this combination of slip-form in the inside and regular forming on the outside.

After that, the cycle of pouring was a 24-hour-a-day process: slipping 16 hours a day, then tying and welding steel, then getting everything set, then resuming after eight more hours. If you look at the tower today you can see the gradations of color caused by the weather being cooler, then warmer. There's a little bit of a different color in the white, then it turns to sort of a gray level, then goes back to a lighter color. It's that little gradation that gives it a very interesting vertical character. That expresses the daily cycle of pouring.

A system of lift-slab jacks raised the unfinished tophouse in 20 days. On facing page, the tower forms a backdrop for the HemisFair visit of President Lyndon B. Johnson on July 4, 1968.

During design we came up with an idea on raising the tophouse. We designed it so the tophouse could be built at the bottom around the shaft and then be lifted up. We didn't dictate any of that, because we didn't want to get into the contractors' business, though the contractors did want to use the basic system we facilitated. It became the logical thing for them to do.

The contractors proceeded with Tex Star Corporation, a company that did a lot of lift-slab work as a contractor and consultant. They designed a system using lift-slab jacks for the tophouse lift. They put 12 of them up on the edges around the top

of the 600-plus-foot shaft and connected them with a kind of a cradle to each of the 24 lifting rods. These were a little over an inch in diameter and of very high strength steel. They dropped the rods all the way down to the tophouse frame at the bottom. At the base the 12 big trusses—which are about 14 feet deep on the inside and come to a thin edge above the observation leve—were assembled and welded together. Then the contractor hooked on to them, and after all were assembled he picked up the whole assembly one floor and hung the next lower floor under that, then picked it up again, and so on.

One cold night before the lift to the top, the rods began to snap on one side of the shaft. The tophouse jerked over about an inch. It was in a precarious position, a whole sector being held by only these two rods, stretched right to their limit. This was October 31, 1967, only about five months until the fair. It was absolutely a critical moment.

The contractor brought in several large mobile cranes from around the state, put them around the structure, reached in, grabbed hold of it and secured it so people would feel comfortable going under it. Then the workmen went under and shored it up, kept it in place. What had happened was that a vibration was set up by the wind in these long rods, and it was all being resolved right above the threads at the bottom. At that point steel would crystallize and break, or fracture. It was clear that this type of rod couldn't be used to lift the tower without risk.

It took maybe a month to figure out what to do. The contractors decided to substitute oil field drill stem pipe for the rods and dampen them every 50 feet by using a device to let it roll on the shaft so that it couldn't vibrate very much. They re-outfitted it with 12 of the pipes instead of the 24 lifting rods. Once they got it all done, it went up to the top in like 20 days, just sailed right along. At this point there were only about three months left until opening day. The tophouse still didn't have glass in it, nor any interior finishes; it was just a bare shape up there in the air. The contactors did an absolutely incredible job of finishing it out in three months—the whole interior, getting the elevators in, getting everything done. It was just amazing.

After it opened, I know that so many people went up in the tower that it not only paid for itself, but, I think, it paid off a little early.

Another issue surrounding HemisFair concerns the design of the Convention Center on the HemisFair site. A local firm was hired by the city to

An extension of the San Antonio River into HemisFair grounds ended in a lagoon at the new convention center. A tile mural done for the fair by Mexico's Juan O'Gorman crowns the facade of what has since been named the Lila Cockrell Theater. The domed arena in the background was razed in 1996 for a convention center expansion that also cut through the arched walkways at right, permitting a further extension of the river.

design the Convention Center to provide one of the entrances to the fair. O'Neil and I would meet and talk about the design. What we saw in the design was something that looked almost like a Texas Highway Department building: porcelain, enamel and glass. It didn't seem to speak to the character of San Antonio on one hand, nor to open itself up in some way so you could come from the center of the city into the fair.

City Council member Lila Cockrell got involved with us, and others also supported us. The result was a decision to redesign, using arches or something to relate the building to San Antonio. All of those things were done. Tommy Noonan was the architect. Given the little time he had and the kind of work he typically did, he made a really good effort, redirected the design and made a lot of difference in the way HemisFair worked.

The San Antonio River was extended into the Convention Center in front of what is now the Lila Cockrell Theater. That was really a key part. Early on, we were hoping that we could relate the fair's water features to the river itself, another notion about how the fair should reflect San Antonio. But it became pretty clear that we couldn't do that directly because the ground elevation of the HemisFair site was too high to get that done. How could we extend the ambience of downtown into the fair?

Between the Convention Center redesign and the river extension, it was done. Al Peery was director of planning for the fair. O'Neil Ford was director of architecture and design. I was hired as the site person to put together an office and hire staff and to begin the work. I stayed there for about five or six months, then I left the fair staff and returned to work with O'Neil to develop the tower.

I don't think the San Antonio we have today would have occurred without the fair, and I don't mean that in a minor way. I think there are major things that happened here because of the fair. One of the simplest to identify is the Convention Center, which probably wouldn't have happened without the fair, the business it brought and the national exposure we got.

A lot of major people came to the city for the first time during the fair. It began a process of people from elsewhere thinking about San Antonio and thinking about the good times they'd had here, thinking about that quaint little river. After a kind of a slow period in 1969 and '70, '71, things began to pick up downtown—hotels, convention business, river development. I think they can all be directly attributed to the fair.

B. J. "Red" McCombs
HemisFair, Lyndon Johnson and Henry Ford II

A longtime auto dealer and multifaceted investor whose holdings once included the National Basketball Association Championship San Antonio Spurs, and who later purchased the Minnesota Vikings, B. J. "Red" McCombs was president of the San Antonio Chamber of Commerce in 1964–65 and served on HemisFair's executive committee as planning began.

As the HemisFair Executive Committee, of which I was a member, began planning to open the fair in the spring of '68, for two and a half to three years before the fair we met five or six days a week every morning at 7:30. These became daily sessions. Each one of us had different areas that we were working in.

One of the things I was asked to chair was the committee on what would be the theme project of the fair. As we all know, it ultimately was the Tower of the Americas. I had a very active committee, some people I had not worked with before, some investment bankers, really bright people. In our planning process, one thing we learned very quickly was that never in the history of the world had a tower been built that was not an economic success.

So we settled on the tower. A person from the side, as it were, who was not on our committee but was well aware of the committee and of our work, was the architect O'Neil Ford. O'Neil was a close personal friend as well as one of the premiere architects, not only in San Antonio but in his time. So O'Neil and I were social buddies as well as having done some business together, and we particularly enjoyed drinking together.

O'Neil was really pressing me to "do a tower," because he wanted to make a statement in concrete. He had this theory that nowhere in the U.S. had anyone really done with cement or concrete all that could be done.

B. J. "Red" McCombs at the time of this photo was a member of HemisFair's executive committee.

And it was such a great source and people in Mexico knew so much more about it than in the U.S., but he really wanted to do a huge shaft of concrete with his little doughnut, as he called it, on top, which ultimately happened.

Pat Zachry, chief executive of H. B. Zachry and Co., was on the executive committee and an officer of the fair. He was a man whom I respected as much and personally liked as much or more than anyone that I ever met in my life, and he was beginning to tell me privately, "I certainly hope you come up with something other than a tower that I keep hearing about, because a tower is ugly. A tower really says nothing, and a tower would be like a 'me-too' project because Seattle had a tower as a focal point."

It was obvious we were headed toward recommending a tower. About two weeks before our deadline, I met privately with Mr. Zachry and told him where we were headed. He was very, very outspoken in his soft, beautiful way: "Red, please, there has to be something that would be a better alternative than that."

And so I suggested to him that, just privately between him and myself, as we had about two weeks left if he could put his staff together and come up with something that maybe I could recommend to my committee other than a tower, I certainly would look at it. He had his staff work out two or three alternatives.

One was something similar to the Tivoli Gardens—a couple or three nice, beautiful, aesthetic kind of projects, but they were costly and would not pay for themselves, although they would have been beautiful within the fair. I just indicated to Mr. Zachry that I was not going to recommend any of those to our committee and that the following week we would recommend the tower to the executive committee, which I felt like it would be tantamount to that being the theme project. So at the executive committee meeting, I gave the report and recommended that the tower be built.

Mr. Zachry made a very eloquent pitch against the tower for all the reasons I've already mentioned. And then, as I recall, the vote was like 10 or 11 to 1. He was the only dissenter. But after the vote was taken, being the gentleman that he was, he rose to his feet and said, "Although I object to this strenuously, I will never publicly make a statement against the tower. I understand majority rules, and so good luck."

We issued 20-year revenue bonds. The revenue sources to the city were greater than what the bonds were, and the bonds were paid off in advance, as I recall. We burned the bonds in about 18 years with a little ceremony at the base of the tower. So the tower was a project that paid for itself, never cost the taxpayers a nickel, and, of course, still stands today as a symbol of San Antonio. And it's still generating revenue.

Getting industrial pavilions was one of the biggest problems we faced in the fair, although there were many, many problems, and I can't say that this was the biggest problem, but this certainly was one of the biggest problems. As a world's fair, we were operating under a charter from the Bureau of International Expositions in Paris.

Under that charter, as a certain class world's fair, we had certain requirements we had to meet. One of those requirements was some 20-odd freestanding, industrial exhibits that would be in buildings that would have to be land leased from the fair corporation. Then the Fortune 500-type company would have to build a building, put a theme in that building compatible to the theme of the fair and then staff that building for a period of six months. So, obviously, this was a very expensive expenditure.

Our basic professional staff had people who were in that business. Most of them had been involved at Seattle's World Fair, which was a success. There was a core of 8 to 10 or 12 of these people who were very talented and were certainly a resource to us. They had been telling us for some time that they were having a very difficult time meeting this particular requirement.

So we came up against a time line problem, meaning we were about to run out of time to get this done. We had one of our very many special-call emergency meetings where Gov. John Connally was called to come down from Austin.

Notwithstanding all the great work that was done by so many people in seeing that the fair was conceived and built and had a successful conclusion—many, many people were involved, particularly, as already mentioned, Marshall

Texas Governor John Connally, shown to the right of President Lyndon Johnson during a visit to HemisFair, provided critical support during fair planning.

Steves and Bill Sinkin—in my personal judgment, the person who had the most influence that absolutely was critical to the times we had problems that we could not solve otherwise was Gov. John Connally.

John was called on this situation and the discussion was, what do we do about it? We were about a year and a half before the fair opened. So we were about to run out of time to get a prospect to come in, build a building, and put a project in it and open with the fair. As I recall we had to have a minimum of 23 to 26, but somewhere over 20. We had gotten 3 of these 20-odd commitments right off. As I recall, they were Southwestern Bell, General Electric and IBM. But once we got those three, we went for like a year without getting any others. So we were nearing the end of the time, and we couldn't yet even qualify to be a world's fair.

We were way deep in the ditch, big time. Governor Connally asked if I would take a special assignment to visit with the staff, and we'd get back together in two or three days and see if we could come up with some solutions. I would have done anything that John Connally asked me to, ever. But in the day I spent going over the fair staff's files and working with the staff, I could not see anything that any prudent person could have done that they had not already done. The bottom line was they didn't have access, because the major corporations in the U.S., in 1966, thought of San Antonio as being something maybe like Laredo or maybe like Abilene. There absolutely was no interest. It was very disheartening to me.

Now, during that same time I personally had been unsuccessful, because I personally had the assignment to deliver Ford Motor Company. And I had a very close relationship with Lee Iacocca established in the '50s, early on in his career and in my career. And here we are up in 1966, and Lee was president of Ford Motor Company and a member of the board and I had pitched him and pitched him, and he was telling me that the company wasn't going to go for it. We were beginning to have cuss fights over the phone and, indeed, also in visits to Detroit.

While I had this assignment and had not yet responded to Governor Connally but had met with the staff, that same afternoon, as ironic as it would seem, I get a call from Iacocca in Detroit. In essence he said, using his typical salty, four-letter language, "I don't want any argument about this. I don't want any backtalk. I don't want any conversation. Here's what's going to happen. We are not going to build a building—period. It's over. It's not going to go any further. Governor Connally is going to get a call from Mr. Ford's office, and Mr. Ford [Henry Ford II] is going to tell him he's going to send a personal emissary down with a check for $250,000 for the governor to buy an art object of his choosing, and that will be Ford Motor Company's gift for the fair."

I immediately started cursing Iacocca. We didn't want the $250,000; we had plenty of art gifts. We had to have the building and the pavilion. He and I are having a cuss fight over the phone when the magic, magic phrase appeared and his response was, "Red, I'm not going to talk about it anymore. I know you're caught up in that dusty, damn little ol' town down there that you think is so world class, but, in the scope of things, there is no political or economic significance to the Ford Motor Company in that fair in San Antonio, Texas."

And suddenly a light came on, and I said, "Good-bye." He said, "Good-bye." I don't know who hung up on the other first.

I immediately called Governor Connally, and I said, "Guess what? We've been trying to sell this thing when the dogs don't like the dog food." I repeated the conversation that I had with Iacocca. He said, "Well, well, well. Well, that's just what we'll do."

He said, "You call Iacocca back and tell him not to worry about that anymore, that I'll call Lyndon, and Lyndon will within 24 hours tell Mr. Ford the political significance of that dusty little town, San Antonio, Texas." And he chuckled. I was delighted.

"I know you're caught up in that dusty, damn little ol' town down there," Lee Iacocca told Red McCombs in explaining why Ford Motor Co. would not have a pavilion at HemisFair.

I called Iacocca, and his secretary, whom I've known for years, said, "Red, I'm sorry, but I'm just going to tell you he does not want to talk to you."

I knew that was probably going to happen, so I knew I had to have a story for her. I told her, " I understand that and I've been out of line. I could understand why he's come to that conclusion, but I called to apologize to him. I have been wrong. Just hook me up to him and let me just apologize to him and put our friendship back in place." She said, "Oh, Red, that is so nice. I'll get him right on the phone." So Iacocca comes on the phone. I apologize profusely. He takes the bait really big and says, "Well, you know, you just pushed too hard. You got out of line."

I said, "But the big thing is, Lee, is that there is a successful conclusion here." I said, "You and I don't have to worry about this. We're out of it. I called Governor Connally and told him you had said that this has no political or economic significance for the Ford Motor Company. And he said for me not to bother with this anymore and to let you know for you not to bother with it, because he would have Lyndon call Henry within 24 hours and explain the political significance of this."

Getting Ford's pavilion opened the way to industrial participation and the fair's success.

Well, Iacocca was stunned. He said, "Oh, you're BS-ing me. You're pulling my chain." And I said, "No, let's don't even worry about it. We're not concerned about this anymore."

Then he started backing up a little, and said, "Well, look, if you're really telling me the truth here, I worked on this so hard for a year and a half. Let me go tell Henry that the president is going to call him."

So that was the way that ended. We found out that we were not going to be able to sell those Fortune 500 companies based upon the fair itself or on the economic interest. Thank God for John Connally and his relationship with President Johnson that we opened the fair with every one of the exhibits that we needed. Mr. Henry Ford came down himself, spent two days, made great speeches about the significance of San Antonio to Ford Motor Company, and a great day was had by all.

When Ford signed up, it didn't only break the ice, then they realized what it was going to take. So then Governor Connally, with President Johnson, began making the calls, and that problem was over. We did qualify with no problem, and the people and the CEOs of those corporations all came to San Antonio and said real good and nice things.

And, you know, the people going to the fair and enjoying the fair never really realized what had happened. But it was absolutely a very, very necessary and significant part of the fair.

But that was not the only role that Governor Connally played. Our fair had to have state participation, which ended up in being the Institute of Texan Cultures. Having said that, the fact that Governor Connally and Senator Ralph Yarborough not only disliked each other, but really, seriously disliked each other, made it a situation to where it took all the finesse there was. In my opinion, no one with any less talent than Governor Connally could ever have pulled all that off.

In those days, the Republican Party didn't exist in Texas. There were conservative Democrats and liberal Democrats; Connally was conservative and Yarborough was liberal, totally opposite poles. And on the other hand, President Johnson had to have his relationship with Senator Yarborough, although, as everyone knew, Governor Connally was one of his closest advisers all of his life. But Governor Connally had that ability to cut through and create things, even with all of these obstacles. I don't believe anyone else in that role could have done it.

So we wound up with state participation. The Institute of Texan Cultures is still going strong, a landmark for San Antonio. It is a component of the University of Texas, funded and kept up by the University of Texas. A lot of citizens are not aware of that, but it is a great contribution from the University of Texas system to San Antonio, and a continuing one, as is the use of the two federal buildings by the federal government after the fair.

HemisFair's Texas Pavilion became the Institute of Texan Cultures, a museum and research center run by the University of Texas.

The Golden Garter, a Western-type saloon, was the "watering hole" for HemisFair.

I think that you could readily see in these two issues that I discussed here specifically, and then in the issues of federal pavilions and state pavilions, that it required an awful lot of decision-making and management, just on the staff of the fair. The core of the staff was hired out of the professionals, as I have already mentioned, who had done other fairs.

But we had to have someone locally who could pull these divergent opinions, and all these areas that none of us knew anything about, together. Frank Manupelli and Jim Gaines were heading up that staff. Jim not only became ill, but also he had some problems with some of the other leadership of the fair, and really didn't get to use all of his management ability. But I watched Frank Manupelli from a day-to-day staff standpoint of working through all these problems.

Here is just one little illustration. Angelo Drossos and I were the very closest of friends. Angelo had a couple of Coney Island hotdog stands downtown that he had inherited from his father. So Angelo tells me early on, when we're planning the fair, that what we've got to do is get the hot dog concession.

Well, I had a conflict of interest, because here I am on the executive committee. But, at that time, I didn't really understand conflict of interest too well, so I go busting in to Manupelli and the other staff people and say, "I want to bid on a concession for hot dog stands with Angelo Drossos and a group of investors."

Well, Manupelli in a very nice, but straightforward way said, "You know, Red, you can't be involved in this at all." So I kept pushing, and this issue was hanging on. One day Manupelli said, "You know, we've got a big problem here that we can't resolve at the moment. We must have a Western-type saloon-type place built to where there is a stage show. We haven't been able to get anybody to agree to do that. If you'll talk to Angelo and your crowd, I might give you a half dozen or so of those hot dog stands, if you guys would agree to build this."

That turned out to be the Golden Garter, which turned out to be the watering hole of the fair.

So I took that idea back to Angelo and he said, "I don't think we can make enough off those hot dogs to pay for the loss on that damn thing." So we began working on it. Finally, the group decided that we would go ahead and do it. It was quite an expensive undertaking. We were just holding our noses about the loss we were going to take on the Golden Garter, but we were going to reap all this money from these hot dogs.

Well, our business expertise turned to be exactly backwards. Those hot dog stands never did even pay for themselves, for reasons I don't know. We ended up closing half of them. And that loser that we thought was going to be the Golden Garter ended up to be a gold mine. That thing just coined money day and night.

So much for all this great business expertise.

2. The Economic Legacy

Once HemisFair energized the business environment, a host of economic developments unfolded. Many of them are recalled here by five business leaders.

Robert F. McDermott: *Economic Development and COPS*

Brig. Gen. Robert F. McDermott (USAF, ret.) came to San Antonio in retirement in 1968 after serving as the first dean of the U.S. Air Force Academy in Colorado Spings. He spent the next 25 years with USAA, serving as chairman and CEO from 1969 to 1993.

I came to San Antonio right in the middle of HemisFair, so I had the opportunity during July and August and September of enjoying all the activities associated with the fair. My feeling, and the feeling of my family at the time, is that we were very lucky indeed to come to such a city, when you think of the three dimensions—a place to work, a place to live, and a place to play. San Antonio had them all, A-pluses. I had never been stationed here. I had occasionally been here on Air Force business at Randolph, but I had no real acquaintance with the town and its activities.

So I had a great orientation during the early HemisFair months. Then when I took over USAA and reality hit home in 1969, I found out that there was no plan for after HemisFair. The city was just kind of applauding itself for a great success. A little bleeding from money lost here and there, but on the other hand, and rightfully so, the community was very happy with what they had accomplished. But there was no follow-up plan whatsoever to take advantage and capitalize on that, in attracting people to come and live here rather than visit here.

So I found a city that was not unlike the one I had left at Colorado Springs, where the Air Force Academy was a city dominated pretty much by military bases and tourism as an industry, very little manufacturing. The economic activity was low, the good, high-paying job opportunities were low. In the first two or three years that I was here, I don't think any significant business moved into San Antonio.

I joined the Chamber of Commerce then, because I felt that was a way to get involved in helping out in some of the things that I'd started doing in Colorado Springs. In Colorado Springs, I associated with a gentleman who ran Command Nuclear. He and I together put together a plan to diversify industry in Colorado Springs, try to bring in some businesses, some high-tech businesses, because, like San Antonio, Colorado Springs didn't enjoy raw materials that would lead to heavy manufacturing or cheap water transportation accessibility, which also leads to heavy manufacturing. So I looked for opportunities to do something to put San Antonio on a course parallel to that of Colorado Springs, in sort of getting a silicon base for economic activity, to give higher and better paying jobs to our population.

The leaders here didn't seem to be receptive; there seemed to be a sleepy attitude. They were sort of taking a sabbatical after HemisFair, and it looked like it was going to go on for years. But on the other hand, there's a

Robert F. McDermott came to San Antonio during HemisFair to join USAA.

lot of satisfaction that they were in a place where there was a lot of retail activity associated with tourists coming in and making purchases here, and a lot of hospitality industry economic activities. A sort of a self-satisfaction that this was a nice, quiet place that everybody wanted to come to. It was the number two city for everybody who lived in the major cities of Texas. So they came in on weekends. I had a hard time getting people interested in economic expansion of the city.

It seemed that the old money wanted to make sure it stayed a quiet city, without strong newcomers and strong new money coming in. In fact, when I went out to raise money to start the Economic Development Foundation, I didn't get any funds from the old families. Most of the interest in the economic development of the city came from *auslanders* like myself, people who had come in here and saw the potential and wanted the city to expand because they thought it had a lot to offer other businesses, particularly in the headquarters area. The high-tech possibility had to be associated with an education base that we didn't have at the time.

But, anyway, what I felt we had to do was develop a plan, stimulate some interest, and I was helped by a negative factor. That was, there was frustration in the business community, the development side of the city was unhappy. The developers were getting together and looking toward a separate chamber of commerce on the North Side. They felt that the downtown chamber was only interested in downtown and historic preservation, and really not much concerned about growth or a new regional airport or any activities that might lead to an explosive development of the city. They were worried about keeping it as a nice place to live.

I think they were mainly people who were in the oil business, the financial business and agri-business. They had made money based here, although their oil drilling took place elsewhere, as some of their ranching and agri-business did. But they were self-satisfied that they were doing well and had a nice place to live in a quiet city, and an easy access to an airport to go wherever they wanted to go when they had the time or on their business.

Now, the other side of it is, there was an interest you'd normally expect among businessmen. The transients who had come here thought this was a great place to live and to work and to play, as did people who'd been here through the military at one time or another and were interested in coming back here. But there were no economic opportunities for them. So, what I did was try to start the ball rolling by getting the Chamber of Commerce to develop a long-range plan.

The chamber, like many businesses, had very different horizons from what one would hope for, and didn't project ahead on a five-year plan, for example, but were only projecting for things going well during the current fiscal year. We worked out a five-year plan, and I thought we were well on the road. But like many other plans that have been developed under Chamber of Commerce auspices, it was well thought out, well researched and well done, and then put in the file.

A year later, I was elected chairman of the chamber for 1974–75. I decided we would start to work the plan, the action programs in the long-range plan, and move toward economic development of the city. That's when the opposition from the North Side group, the developer's group, became a little heated. I thought there was all the more reason that we had to have this or we were going to split the city of San Antonio into several chambers, each working on its own segment of the city. The overall umbrella had to be an Economic Development Foundation.

Starting the Economic Development Foundation

So I started an Economic Development Foundation and went out personally and raised money, over a period of about a month, from 29, as I recall, businesses, mostly run by *auslanders*. I was looking for a half million dollars. I was following a similar plan Atlanta had used in what they called "The Forward Atlanta Movement." They had a $600,000 pledge for three years from their business community. As a smaller city I set a goal of $500,000; we got $540,000 with three-year pledges.

We then went out, and methodically I went down the course that Atlanta had led for us. We hired the same public relations company, Manning, Selvage and Lee. And then we hired the Fantis Corp., the major relocation firm in the United States. They helped companies choose by assessing cities for their economic development potential, and helped companies relocate or locate plants or regional offices.

When that study was made, copies were given to all of the investors of the Economic Development Foundation. I sent one to Mayor Lila Cockrell, who read that and was intrigued by it. She allowed the young council member named Henry Cisneros to read it. And Henry made copies of some of the pages in that master document, and that came back to bite us in our development. I'll get to that when I get around to discussing the Communities Organized for Public Service.

Suffice it to say, at this point, that we were off to a good start. We had the money, like Atlanta had when they started their movement. We had a three-year pledge. We had pulled the business community together, both the North Side chamber members and the Greater San Antonio chamber members, and there was some excitement about the opportunities we might have ahead to develop along the plan laid out in the master document by the Fantis Corp. They evaluated our assets and our liabilities and recommended what industries would most likely succeed in San Antonio's economic environment, given the limitations the city had in terms of water transportation and raw materials, given the opportunities it had with air transportation and high-value, low-volume items that could be air transportable.

Clearly that led us into, as a major thrust, the kind of companies that located around Palo Alto and around the University of Texas—the microelectronics, microchip companies that were high-paying, high-tech job opportunities. That also gave us an obligation to do something about our educational opportunities in the city, to prepare people to work in those kind of companies, and for professionals in that kind of business to upgrade themselves, given the rapid changes in technology that were exploding all over the country.

One of the assets that the Fantis report highlighted was that we had a low cost of living and relatively cheap labor, and, therefore, a company moving in would have lower costs manufacturing here. You might parallel it today to the outsourcing that takes place from the United States to Taiwan or Latin America. At that time, taking a purely economic view of the situation, it looked like San Antonio was a great place for outsourcing from high-labor-cost areas like California.

Dealing with Communities Organized for Public Service

However, placing an accent on that statement, mention in the Fantis report about an economic advantage and having cheap labor raised the ire of those who were followers of the Saul Alinsky movement, in San Antonio an organization called Communities Organized for Public Service. Henry Cisneros, as a young councilman, passed on to COPS those pages of the Fantis report. That led to the shocking confrontation I had with COPS in October 1977, at St. Mary's Immaculate Church, when Father Albert Benavides confronted me as the man who was advocating that companies bring in low-paying jobs to San Antonio.

His presentation was accented by the fact that *Newsweek* magazine said the average family income in the United States at that time was $15,000 a year and that the Mexican American community was not going to accept any below-average jobs, that their time had come and they were demanding jobs paying no less than the average. They had to make up for the past.

While I was on stage with Father Benavides, it was one of those situations of sticking a mike in your face, asking you a question and then pulling the mike back and giving you yes or no answers. And giving you no opportunity to address the crowd or to educate them in any way. When they were through with their scenario, the meeting was over. And they walked out.

I knew about the Saul Alinsky movement, the *Rules for Radicals* book written by Saul Alinsky, and some of his recommended tactics. So I knew what was going on, but there was nothing as a sole enemy in the room that I could do about it. I might just as well have had hydrophobia.

I went back then to the business community of San Antonio. None of them appeared to know anything about the Industrial Area Foundation of Saul Alinsky or his books or his movement. So I tried to buy some and I couldn't find any in San Antonio. I went to Austin and bought all the copies that were available in the bookstore up there and brought them down and passed them out for reading in the San Antonio business community so they would be aware of what we were up against.

What happened was that they did exactly what was in the textbook, for example like going to Frost Bank and changing pennies to dollars and dollars back to pennies, then going to Joske's and trying on clothes, one garment after another, so they'd be soiled. The fact that it happened according to the textbook got everybody alerted to the fact that, "Yeah, this is an economic reality."

The other thing they were able to do is they would call the press ahead of deadline time and say there's going to be such and such happening at Frost Bank or such and such happening at the telephone company at 10 o'clock, and be there and we'll put on a show for you.

This went on for a brief period and then, following my recommendation, the business community shut down access to their property. Then after a stalemate period, and I can't remember how long it was, with no economic activity, I accented the facts that Alan Bradley, a manufacturing company like John Deere which was coming in here, stopped their movement into San Antonio because of this confrontation and moved to South Carolina. Texas Instruments was coming here, and they went to Colorado Springs.

At that time there was an article in a magazine, I think it was *Texas Monthly,* about Henry Cisneros and Raza Unidas. The gentleman from Texas Instruments came in, showed me that cover and said, "You know, with this possibility that Raza Unidas will take over San Antonio, I'm sorry, but we are not going to move into your city." And in fact, they did not. So we lost two good prospects.

I fell back and regrouped and thought, well, what'll I do now? I'll do the very thing they need the most, bring new jobs into town, higher paying jobs, and they've killed it, they've shot themselves right in the foot, both feet. But how can you, when you're working against a propaganda philosophy advanced by Saul Alinsky, win? Except making them face reality? And the reality was no jobs came in.

Having shut them off of communications—and they were very anxious to communicate with me then—I negotiated that I would meet with them in a small group and try to educate them on my side of the picture and give them an opportunity for them to educate me on their side of the picture.

We set up a format where there were four on my side of the table—myself, Bob West, who was head of Tesoro Petroleum; Harold O'Kelley, who was head of Datapoint; and Ralph Thomas, who was the Economic Development executive vice president. On the COPS side of the fence, Father Benavides was the leader of the delegation, although he listed himself as the adviser, and it was the president of COPS and two vice presidents. This was maybe a year and a half after the big confrontation, and no new jobs or new companies had come into San Antonio in the meantime.

Dennis Donovan, executive head of the Fantis Corp., came in to try to educate them on what they said in their master report document and what it meant and why. They were completely intolerant of anything he had to say, and it turned out to be another confrontation. So that's what finally killed it. He couldn't convince them that the plan that they outlined was the way for us to go, so he pulled out.

Unfortunately, out of that we got national headlines in *Forbes* magazine, and that really closed us down. Once we hit the national headlines, that cut San Antonio out of the picture as a prospect for economic development.

So then I tried the "old dean's approach." I set up a series of meetings with them where I would share time and we'd alternate. I'd make my presentations and let them make theirs so we could arrive at an understanding. We finally arrived at a treaty, after a year, that we would work together and not apart. They understood my point of view or the business community's point of view, and I understood theirs. And I did understand that they wanted to be a part of the economic development process and know about it ahead of time and be apprised of what was planned and what was going on.

For my part, I tried to educate them on the fact that we didn't have the educational level or the skill worker level to bring in jobs that would result in average family income for our city. For one thing, our families were larger, and for another thing our wages were lower for many reasons. Wages were much lower in all categories, all levels of employment here than, say, in the Northeast, in any of the manufacturing or service industries. I showed them appropriate charts that San Antonio had one of the lowest levels of education—that's graduation from high school—and one of the worst drop-out rates of any of the 12 major cities. And high illiteracy.

I pointed out that what they should be working on so that we could work together was to work on education and the K through 12 level, keeping kids in school and improving the schools and the education so that kids could indeed aspire to better jobs, more high-paying jobs, following education with training in the high-tech area. EDF's responsibility was bringing in jobs.

The United San Antonio Movement

This was in the fall of '79. As we moved along, having these sessions at some frequency, I, in turn, was out working to bring in companies. Finally, I launched something called the United San Antonio Movement in January 1980. The purpose of that movement was to identify issues that would adversely affect the economic development of our city, and get together and work out action programs to correct those deficiencies and positively to work out advantages, work out plans to promote the advantages we had over other cities—not to sell the town as a low-wage or cheap labor town, but to sell the city of San Antonio as one that was addressing its problems and one that had a bright future because we were pulling together, we were united.

Along the way we made another convert—the young city councilman who handed over the inflammatory material to COPS became one of our best economic development salesmen, Henry Cisneros. The way that happened is, in an unusual troika I divided the leadership for this movement into three classes: the business class, which is obvious; the political class, which is politicians at any level; and the public sector I identified as citizens.

What I tried to do, myself taking on the position of the chairman of the business sector, was to get Lila Cockrell to appoint for me, representing the government sector, a young councilman who was by far the brightest star in San Antonio in the government sector, and she did. So Henry Cisneros became one of the tri-chairmen.

The third one I went for was Archbishop Flores, who was relatively new to the city. I thought he would be an ideal selection to represent the community at large, what I call the public sector. He decided not to accept that position. After discussions with Lila and Henry, we picked Dr. San Jose Martin, a professional man, an optometrist who had his own business, had done a tour as a councilman and represented the minority side.

We identified 14 issues or problem areas for focus group development. We always looked for tri-chairs on each committee so that we would have African American, Hispanic and Anglo represented. The water issue would have a focus group—crime, downtown redevelopment, you name it, we had identified all the issues and lined up the focus groups, asked everyone to participate in one or more focus groups where they felt they could make a contribution, either in identifying the issue or in solving the problem.

One of my problems all my life has been a 16-hour day. But I'm just a workaholic, I guess. That's the main reason I was able to do it. I certainly didn't neglect my company; I grew it at a fantastic rate over that period.

The change from confrontation to cooperation was dramatically illustrated when members of COPS were present when the governor signed an education reform bill in 1984, the most memorable example I'd seen of the total change in approach to the economic development of San Antonio. What I learned out of the whole thing, and I think the whole business community did, is that we have to work with neighborhoods.

We just can't think that as an economic power bloc we can make things happen in our city. You've got to work bottom-up. And so the focus group approach is the best way to go to get people involved—not just a group that might have a special philosophy, say like the Saul Alinsky group, and a special set of tactics that they think can most appropriately get things done in their behalf, but to get everybody in the spirit of the Golden Rule.

So if you can get people working from that philosophic base, looking out rather than looking in, then I think you can get things moving along, and we did. So COPS came in, although the interesting thing is they're pretty loyal to Alinksy's doctrine "don't ever join a group, always sit on the outside." They would come to our focus group meetings and sit there, but they wouldn't join in, they wouldn't sign up as an organization or as individuals. But in their hearts they were satisfied that things were going the way they would like them to go.

Number one: the formal treaty was certainly one important bit of evidence that they were going to cooperate. Number two: in fact, they did, and they helped other people understand how important, in reaching out to the communities, it was for them to help themselves as well as for us to help them or dictate their futures.

That cooperation is still there, and the enlightenment for the business community is there, too.

Tom C. Frost Jr.: *Development and Consensus*

Civic Leader Tom Frost is senior chairman of Frost National Bank, which was founded by his great-grandfather, and chairman and CEO of its Cullen-Frost Bankers holding company.

Since I came out of school in 1950, my first and only job was with the Frost National Bank. I'm senior chairman of the bank. At that time Frank Gillespie was putting together the Good Government League. Together with a number of civic leaders, he had set up the Research and Planning Council. They brought the city manager/council government to San Antonio. I was not a part of that, but I was a young man able to watch and see what really transpired from the time I graduated in 1950 up until '68.

The Good Government League was still the dominant influence in the community, because they carried all of the city elections and, in effect, had all segments of the community—blacks and Mexican Americans and all the rest—represented in the government. There was a small group within the Good Government League that everybody knew was picking the candidates. They conducted the elections, and the city was really well run. We were the bank for the city and I'd say up until '68 we had a hierarchical government, run by people from the business community.

By the time 1968 came and the planning for HemisFair, Walter McAllister was mayor and was the chief executive officer of the City of San Antonio. We had a very good representative government. As our founding fathers envisioned, we elected people considered to be honest and hardworking. They were of the community, and we allowed them then to run the government of the city. It was done that way and done very well.

I have to say that 1968 is the most important year in the history of San Antonio, even since the coming of the Spaniards and the fall of the Alamo and all the other events. And the reason I say that is the zenith of the representative government under the Good Government League really was attained in 1968. In April of that year we inaugurated HemisFair, which provided the facilities for the tourist industry that now is, I believe in my mind,

the largest single civilian employer in this community.

Also, in September of that year, the first student was admitted to the medical school out in the Medical Center. That, of course, was the genesis of the health care industry which today hires as many civilians as the federal government in Bexar County.

When I say federal government, I'm not including just the Department of Defense. That would include the post office and all the other Feds—the FBI—and my memory is that we're somewhere around 40,000 or so. Health care is about that number. The numbers you have from hotels and restaurants and things like that gets up over 50,000 for the convention/tourist industry.

Those two events were really significant in that years later we're living off of those because the two major employers are health care and the tourist, convention, visitor industry. They were both brought about through the planning and the developments under the

Banker Tom C. Frost Jr.

aegis of the Good Government League.

But one significant thing that brought about a significant political change and a social change was that HemisFair was the first major project I had ever been a part of that involved all segments of the community.

It was actually proposed by Henry Gonzalez, who stood in the liberal element of the Democratic Party. It was supported by Mayor McAllister, who was one of the few Republicans in the community at that time. It was also supported strongly by Gov. John Connally, who was the kingpin of the conservative wing of the Democratic Party. So, politically we had all aspects represented.

Then we had, for the first time in my career, labor unions on board, and they were supporting the fair. Startlingly, we had women on the board. It was also one of the first major elements where we found civic leaders in the persons of Nancy Negley, George Brown's daughter; Reagan Houston's wife Mary Jane; and Jessica Catto. These I remember offhand who formed integral parts in the governing groups of HemisFair. And we had people from both the Hispanic and the black community on the board.

So the interesting thing here is that the hierarchial process of representative government and management of the city through Good Government League not only brought about these significant events, but brought about the first step that led toward what I call the participatory democracy we are working under in San Antonio in a very successful way today. All elements of the community have a participation in the governing process, even in the civic, economic development process, which they did not enjoy under a representative government. HemisFair was the hallmark of that.

Decision-making for HemisFair vs. the Medical Center

There's an interesting paradox in this, in that the Medical Center and the way it was located was exactly the opposite of that. It was decided by a small group of people who still meet today—different people—the Board of Regents of the University of Texas, and through its leadership in San Antonio offering it to them.

There was a significant controversy here over the location of the Medical Center, and it quite divided the city, including the business community, as to whether it should be located downtown near the then-only public hospital—the Robert B. Green—or out on the new campus, where it was. That was the last real bitter difference we had in San Antonio, among ourselves on a significant project, and I think most of that scar has healed over.

The County Commissioners Court, that passes tax assessments, would make the money available for the teaching hospital. The Hospital District was involved because of the requirement of the University of Texas that the local community provide the facility of a teaching hospital. The community was ready to do that through the Hospital District and what was then the Robert B. Green, now called University Hospital out there; the Green exists as a downtown kind of clinic.

Anyway, the Commissioners Court was going to have to take that vote. The Commissioners Court consists of four commissioners and the county judge. Two commissioners were split, so it was 2 to 2. The deciding ballot was going to be the county judge, Blair Reeves. I was a part of a group put together by John Peace, who was on the Board of Regents, to call on Bruzzie Reeves and give him the support to vote "yes" and be the swing vote. He was really on the hot spot. Was he going to double our taxes on the Hospital District and bring about the medical school, or was he going to force the issue that we wouldn't, and perhaps take the risk that we bring the medical school here but bring it downtown? They got the larger taxpayers of the community to go see him. Frost Bank was second largest, next to Southwestern Bell, in being taxed on real estate.

So I went to that meeting and H. B. Zachry was at that meeting. My father and Pat Zachry were two of those who thought it was better to have the hospital downtown, so the community wouldn't have to support two teaching hospitals. The decision was obvious from the Board of Regents that they were either going to go out on a new campus, where it is now, north of town, or not come at all.

I came back from Austin from a meeting of the Board of Regents I attended as a guest, or a public participant, and told my father that there was no question in my mind that we either made a choice—we either built the second hospital and got the medical school and the Medical Center or we didn't, and then we didn't get the medical school or the Medical Center. I can remember his decision was, well, while that's a more costly way to do it, it certainly is better in the long run to do that than let the thing go.

Mr. Zachry led the charge. I was there when he made the presentation to the Board of Regents of $1 million in cash to buy the land to bring them down in the Urban Renewal District downtown. Half a million of that was a check, a cashier's check of the Frost Bank, and a half a million was a check of the National Bank of Commerce. So there was unity in the downtown group in favor of downtown. But Mr. Zachry also had come around, and he led the group that went there—I was a part of it.

I can remember going to Bruzzie Reeves and telling him what benefit we thought would come to the city, and that it was up to this or nothing. As an aside, I'll say that none of us realized how significant it was going to become. But we told him that we wanted him to vote for it. We also were coached by John Peace that the thing we needed to say was that we know this is a political risk and we will pledge to you support, including financial support, in your next election. We're the largest taxpayers in town, and everybody isn't just going to run from you and leave you out in the open once you make the vote.

I'll give Bruzzie Reeves a lot of credit, because he could have voted no and probably stayed in office real easy. He looked at us and said, "You're right, it will be a benefit to this community. We should have it. And your pledge to support me gives me the ability to vote for it." And he went and voted for it. And he really gets the hero's reward. But it needs to be known that he was given a little backbone, that the large taxpayers were not going to abandon him and would say publicly with him, "We will accept a doubling of our taxes because this is good for the community."

These two events, the medical school and HemisFair, brought about by a more hierarchical representative government, have led us to a transition to participatory democracy. One by a success, HemisFair showing that by bringing everyone together we can build things, and the Medical Center showing the risks of the failure of not working together. It also led to an interesting step forward to where the chief economic development officer of San Antonio is now the mayor.

I'm leaping forward, but I'll have to tell you my personal experience in bringing the North American Development Bank to San Antonio is that there was a whole wide spectrum of people from the Southwest Voter Institute, the Mexican American Legal Defense Fund and La Raza Unida who worked together with the Chamber of Commerce, the Economic Development Foundation and all of the business community to make our offer and make it available to the North American Development Bank and bring it here. So together we can move mountains.

The North American Development Bank is a multilateral, multinational governmental bank set up where 50 percent is owned by the government of Mexico, 50 percent by the government of the United States, passed at the same time we passed the North American Free Trade Agreement and dedicated to financing environmental infrastructure and environmental projects on the border. The governments of Mexico and the United States have thereby put their seal of approval on endorsing San Antonio, as a place to do business between the two countries. As we aspire to another goal, to become a center of trade with the Americas beginning with Mexico, this is a significant endorsement of this community by the two governments.

In moving from a hierarchically managed type of government to a participatory government in which everyone has their say, the mayor is no longer in the position that Walter McAllister was, of calling all the shots and being responsible for the naming of all of his councilmen and women. Now single-member districts and the entire town feels they have the ability to influence what the city does, or least to have some input.

We've accomplished it because there were significant people, particularly Hispanics who've been put in high positions. The first one is Henry Gonzalez; we owe a significant debt to him. He is a watershed event like HemisFair and the medical school, and I hope that in the future they look upon the North American Development Bank as a watershed event.

How "Us" Prevailed over "Us or Them"

Henry Gonzalez was the first Mexican American elected to a high political position here in modern times. He could have taken the position at the time of an "us or them." I heard him say to a group of his supporters in the Convention Center after HemisFair, "We cannot set ourselves apart. To enjoy the benefits of society, one must participate in society and be a part of it."

If Henry Gonzalez had taken a different position before he was elected, there would have not been a HemisFair. Henry Gonzalez was the person who called the first meeting to even discuss HemisFair. And he said, "I think I can convince Congress that they should put a pavilion in a fair honoring the confluence of the civilizations, if the business community would like to support it and we'd commemorate our anniversary that way." That was a pre-'68 watershed event that, then, also was significant in moving toward participatory democracy.

The other person I will give real kudos to for making that move gracefully in San Antonio is Lila Cockrell. Lila Cockrell was mayor at the time we went to city single-member districts. The pitfall that we could have fallen into was that councilpersons could have acted in ways to divide the city. It almost started out that way. You had people who really didn't know what their allegiance was to the whole and how they should handle themselves and be responsible to their own districts.

Lila Cockrell sat back and smiled an awful lot through some pretty hectic City Council meetings. Through her steady hand she got the City Council people down to realizing, after the first couple of years, that they had to work together and it was better to work together. She endorsed Henry Cisneros as mayor following her, and she handed to Henry a City Council that did understand how to work together, handed him a city that had been brought about by Henry Gonzalez's position, that we're better off staying together and not working apart.

Then Henry Cisneros got 92 percent of the popular vote from all sides of the city because he also said a very significant thing, that the people in this community need jobs and they need better jobs. Those jobs will come from business, so if we can figure out how the city can support the growth and development of business, we'll move forward together. And the community bought that idea. That brought the business community and, we'll say, the economically disenfranchised, together. He was probably the single most important factor in putting San Antonio on the national map.

During this time period, the confrontation between Communities Organized for Public Service and Economic Development Foundation ended as the neighborhood groups seemed to realize that if the jobs were going to be there, someone had to bring them to town and develop them.

I talked to Ernie Cortes one day, and I said, "Ernie, now when you came to town with COPS, I went and ran and got a book of Alinsky's *Rules for Radicals*. I read that because that was your textbook, and let me tell you, you performed perfectly, 100 percent, under that. I could tell what you were doing, when you were going to do it, and it helped me cope with it. I spread it around the business community, and it helped us understand what you were doing, and why, and I think contributed a lot to San Antonio being able to cope with what you did.

"Now, what I want to ask you is this: The confrontation seems to be over with. I'm seeing COPS being in a consultative position with the business community and the rest of the community still maintaining their independence, but it's one of cooperation rather than confrontation. What I need you to tell me is, where is that next book that I ought to be reading so I can understand it and see what you're doing?"

And he said, "Tom, I guess it's being written."

And I said, "Well, I think I'm talking to the author."

And he said, "Yes."

So what happened was that there was an adroit management of the Alinsky process by Ernie Cortes. They had to start out where they had to start out, to get recognition and establish themselves with some immediacy as a force. Then they were smart enough make that change. I think their own membership fed back to them the confrontation and the loss of that one electronic prospect through their confrontation with EDF. There was a bond issue that a confrontation also negated, but I think it was the EDF thing, and the job situation. I think Ernie was sensitive enough to feel that feedback and said, "Wow, we don't want to be a part of chasing jobs off; we want to bring jobs."

So COPS has now been a positive force in many ways, but they have translated their relationship to the rest of the community, particularly the business community, as one of working together.

"And they lived happily ever after" is the way I'd like to hear this story end.

Charles E. Cheever Jr.: *Sharing Power*

Charles E. Cheever Jr. is chairman of Broadway Bancshares Inc. and is a past president of the Greater San Antonio Chamber of Commerce.

If you asked me what has affected San Antonio the most since I've been living in San Antonio permanently since 1957, I would say it is HemisFair. I wasn't as involved in HemisFair as much as one might think, primarily because, at the time, I was on the Board of Managers of the Bexar County Hospital District and then later became chairman, which we'll go into later.

I think that HemisFair really turned downtown San Antonio around. I mean, it really made downtown San Antonio. I was impressed with the way people worked together. You remember Bill Sinkin was one of the driving forces, and Bill was one of the most liberal political people in town. Some of the establishment didn't have much use for Bill, but Bill had a vision, I think, for HemisFair, and he had Henry B. Gonzalez's ear.

Everybody worked real hard and the banks worked together. We put together a loan program, I think it was $5.8 million, and got pledges from businesses to the tune of $7 million to make that loan against. All the banks participated in accordance with their size, and I don't think they thought they were going to lose anything. They didn't, as a matter of fact. But I think everybody went into it with a positive attitude and with an attitude that the visitor projections could be met, which they weren't.

I was the vice chairman with Pat Legan of what they called Visitors Services. Our job was to inventory all the possible housing, they call it

B&B now, but at that time we were just trying to get people to give bedrooms in their homes and serve breakfast.

Gen. Bob Colglazier was the executive director, and he's a very organized guy. He'd done well in the Army and Logistics Command, and so we  had inventoried I don't remember how many homes, with telephone numbers and rates and how many people they would take, would they take kids, would take pets—all the way to Seguin, New Braunfels, Boerne. The idea was that the hotels were going to be filled all the time, and people would have a number to call Visitors Services and we would assign them a place. We didn't get as many people as we were prepared for. And I guess part of that was that San Antonio was kind of unknown in '67, '68.

At the same time the Medical School debate was going on. I got asked to be on the board of managers of the Hospital District in 1961 by Sam Jorrie, who was a county commissioner. My recollection is that the board was either six or seven people, and each commissioner had an appointee. It wasn't supposed to be that way under the law, but it was like districting-in-advance. They appointed us and we were supposed to be fairly independent, but they didn't want us to be too independent.

Banker Charles Cheever Jr.

It was annual begging sessions with Commissioners Court to get enough money to operate the Robert B. Green. I hate to admit this publicly, but I was fairly young at the time. I was 33 when I got appointed, and was looking to a lot of guidance from guys like Leslie Neil and Jim Hollers and people in the Medical Foundation, in medical politics and medical development. I got a lot of advice from them, and normally followed that advice.

But when the battle came to the idea of founding the medical school in San Antonio and it was finally authorized by the Legislature, one restriction was that there had to be a teaching hospital within a mile radius. There was a group of people who desperately wanted it to be downtown near the county's Robert B. Green Hospital for the basis of downtown development and being near the poor, the users of the hospital and all that. In hindsight, there was not enough land available downtown, but I think at the time people thought there was enough land that could be condemned.

The other group had a big constituency. Their pitch was that since this could be the nucleus of a very large medical center, you needed acreage and you needed a nice site and a pleasant site and you needed it not being in downtown San Antonio. As I recall we on the board of managers were tugged back and forth on this thing and there was feeling both ways on the board. But in the long run we didn't have a lot to say about it, since it was going to be a University of Texas facility and went through the Legislature, which decided it was going to be on what we called the Oak Hills site. I remember a lot of controversy, and in fact I got high blood pressure over that thing and ended up resigning in '67 after we had broken ground. But there was a lot of tugging and fighting. I think the hero of that deal was Blair Reeves, who was then the county judge.

The deal was that the University of Texas and the Texas Legislature were putting pressure on the Hospital District to increase services tremendously and to build this new hospital. It couldn't be done without either doubling the tax rate or doubling the assessments, which is the same thing. So it was put to a referendum, and it was defeated.

Then a new bill was introduced by University of Texas proponents to allow Commissioners Court to double the assessment. Blair Reeves, after the voters had turned the deal down, rose to the occasion and said, "In spite of that, I know what's good for San Antonio. I'm going to vote for it." He was the deciding vote. It was a tough vote. As buildings came out of the ground and the people saw how much the University of Texas was putting into our community, I think they forgave him, and he never lost an election.

So in my opinion HemisFair was the most important thing in the period we're talking about, and the Medical Center is the second most important thing.

Is San Antonio a more participatory city than when I came here in '57? No question about it. I mean, 500 percent more. The only thing that troubles me is in a book I would recommend a reading, *The Disuniting of America*, by a well-known liberal writer who bemoans that perhaps the pendulum has swung so far on this diversity thing that we're going to end up being another Bosnia. I worried a little bit in the 1980s and 1990s that instead of integrating we're going toward more separatism. I do think that HemisFair at least started getting everybody working to be more inclusive.

Single-member districts could be either admired as diversity or be concerned about the Balkanization of San Antonio. I think it's been good and bad. The good is that it did pretty well assure that you could get minority candidates elected, whereas prior to that time you couldn't. That was a healthy thing. The weakness, or the bad part of it is, unfortunately, the ward politics. Now you've got ten districts, and if we've got some money we're going to divide it ten ways, that kind of thing.

Sharing Power and Avoiding Violence

Part of how San Antonio escaped the urban violence or the racial violence that other large cities have gone through is the sharing of the power that started in the mid-'60s with HemisFair. Part of it is that in Los Angeles and Detroit it was a black versus Anglo thing, and in San Antonio the primary minority is Hispanic. Hispanics and Anglos are closer on a lot of social and cultural and family and issues than Anglos and blacks. I think that COPS came into town and started out as a radical organization and converted the business community into living together, first cautiously and now a lot better, with the same interests in job development, neighborhood improvement and education.

I'm the chairman of Project Quest, and at the COPS convention Sunday they asked me one of those leading questions: "Mr. Cheever, do you support increasing the Project Quest intake to where there would be a thousand people being trained at the same time, or does business support it?"

After I gave a little preamble about how it was COPS's 20th anniversary and things had certainly changed from the days when Ernie Cortes appeared with *Rules for Radicals* and all that stuff, I said yes. And I said the reason is because what's good for COPS is good for business, what's good for business is good for COPS. The response was good. Then Gov. Ann Richards got up to talk and said, "Well, Charlie said something insightful. What COPS wants is good for business and what business wants is good for COPS. So it is a positive thing."

William E. (Bill) Greehey: *Development and Energy*

William E. Greehey is chairman of Valero Energy Corp.

When I came to San Antonio in 1979 to help set up Valero Energy Corp., maybe 100 people came along. I think we have 700 people in San Antonio, about 1,700 total. We're in three businesses. One is natural gas pipeline; we buy, sell, transport natural gas. The second is natural gas liquids. As the gas moves through our pipeline we put processing plants that extract the natural gas liquids from that natural gas stream and the natural gas liquids I'm talking about—ethane, propane, butane, natural gasoline.

Business leader Bill Greehey.

The third business that we're in is the refining business; we have a refinery in Corpus Christi.

When we came to San Antonio there was a group that represented the North Side. They put a big push on us to put our office building on the North Side of town. Then there was a downtown group that put the big push on us to build downtown. When we decided on this location halfway between we didn't please anybody.

What I saw was a business community that was really divided. You had a strong North Side, primarily the developers, and then you had a strong downtown group. The other thing that I saw was a community that I felt really wasn't working together. You had the COPS group, always at odds with the business community on issues. You had a City Council that was divisive, I thought. You know when you have Bennie Eureste tell me that we can take our company and move it out of San Antonio and you can take the Spurs and leave, you don't have a good council.

What I've seen over the years is a community that has really come together. Business leaders, community leaders, elected officials, COPS, everyone seems to be working together for the common good of San Antonio. I think there've been a lot of new businesses in San Antonio, and there's been a lot of new leadership, and I think that's helped. I think Valero was a big plus coming to San Antonio. Up until Southwestern Bell we were the largest public company here.

One of our missions was to be involved in the community and be community leaders, giving both financially and giving of our time. I feel very strongly that when you have employees that care about the community, really care, they're going to care about the people they work with and they're going to care about the company and they're going to be a lot more productive, with the right attitudes.

I think that's certainly been true in our company. The morale in our company has always been very good. We have not had any turnover; turnover costs you money. Employees have great pride in the company for our community involvement and things that we do. And everything that we've done, we've done consistently.

Also, we're very active on the political scene at the state level, at the national level, within the community. There are several factors in whether we back a political candidate. From a practical standpoint, most of them really don't have that strong of a position on energy. So we look at a person's qualifications, and what their agenda is.

I'm strictly an independent, I'm not a Democrat, I'm not a Republican. I've had fund-raisers for Democrats. I've had fund-raisers for Republicans. I look at who the best person is for the job and that's what our PAC does. But it really is to encourage good people to run and get the best representation you can.

I've been involved in two real controversial issues. One was the Alamodome, and one was the Water Now Campaign. And I found them easy to work with. I think when you really sit down and people talk, everybody wants the same thing. But I think the community is just working great together. I've never seen anything as positive. The dome, I know that was controversial, there's a lot of negative thoughts on that, but you talk to Bob Lanier, who was the mayor of Houston. He would have given anything to have a domed stadium like ours in downtown Houston. I talked to Dallas people, they would give anything to have a domed stadium like ours.

But San Antonio is one place that wherever you go people say San Antonio seems to have its act together, and you're getting things done.

H. Bartell Zachry Jr.: *A Different Community*

Bartell Zachry is chairman of H. B. Zachry Co.

Certainly for San Antonio 1968 was a watershed year, in that it did a lot of building and had participation from a lot of parts of the city. It positioned the city in some ways that I'm not sure that the city would ever have

Contractor Bartell Zachry.

achieved without that, like urban renewal and the things that went with it. And it freed some entrepreneurial spirit that may not have emerged if it hadn't been for HemisFair.

It changed the way things were done in San Antonio, because of the increasing participation. It seems to me that the Good Government League was pretty much wrapping up its activities, because that was personified with Walter McAllister toward the end of his leadership as mayor. I'm not sure whether HemisFair would have been built quite the way it was now if it didn't have a few people who could spearhead and move some things at that time. But at any rate, they got together for the interest of the city. And I think that did a lot.

Individually, I was not really involved in the fair, so my experience is as much from visiting with my father from time to time. He was chairman of the company before me and a prime mover in HemisFair. We had a wonderful father-son relationship. Beyond that, in our business he was marvelous because he was like a partner, and we could divide up certain areas in which we were involved. My brother was in another area of interest.

HemisFair really took all of his time, a lot of his time, and so, since I was president of our construction company from 1965 on, he was really not involved in any construction activities, basically, except the Hilton Hotel itself some. I did not get involved much with San Antonio, so my knowledge of the fair was really more through visits with him and his assessment, what I read in the paper, and in the section on the fair in the book that Amado Cavazos wrote about him, which came out of a lot of his files that he wrote and saved and maintained on the fair.

When I think of the increased number of interests made possible by virtue of that fair, they began, to me, with various people positioning in regard to what was going to happen with the fair after it was over. A lot of dreaming by various constituencies about what could be done began to involve broader areas of the city. Tourism began to play an increasing role, because we now had a convention center we didn't have before. Certainly, our own company's interest changed, because we were also now a majority owner of a hotel property, the Hilton Palacio del Rio.

The hotel construction operation, my father pretty much lived throughout. His offices were downtown and mine were out at our construction office. My role was to see that the project received the support it needed and people and resources. But in terms of working with the city and other things, that was my father's role. But he said when he needed something, it was my job to see that he got it.

The hotel was built by CMI—Concrete Modules, Inc., but we were involved in the process. We built a million-dollar motel on Padre Island. It was cast on shore and went across by barge to Padre Island, so we'd had some experience with doing this before. It was not just created out of a dream. When the question came up to build this facility for the fair, when the property was put together, there was only so much time, and you had limited access to the property because it was on the river. Because of the shortage of time to get it ready—it seems to me we had around nine months to get the project ready—there wasn't a way to do that in that length of time except to try to attack the project from more than one dimension, or direction, at the same time.

That gave rise to the application of what we'd done on the motel to a hotel instead. Getting the design and all of that together and doing it and working the shifts, it was just a major undertaking. But we put a casting yard out on the south side of town, where we have our construction offices, and that's where we cast the facilities. They were completed as a full box, which means that you have double floors, double walls and ceiling, plumbing, electricity and everything installed. As a matter of fact, my wife, Molly, and I rode up in the first box as it was set. We broke the champagne bottle and effectively did the ritual "sign in" of the first guests in the hotel. But anyway, that was the first use of that box.

Subsequently, deciding what to do with the fair property took a while. In retrospect, I'm not so sure it's all bad, because what we would have done then, maybe, would not have fit what it might serve today. We could not have envisioned exactly what this might come to—certainly not a dome. And perhaps the need and different dimensions for that land that would have otherwise been utilized for something else.

I think the fair led to a lot of things. Politically, I think the single-member City Council districts did something for San Antonio. Henry Cisneros did a tremendous amount for this city because he put Target '90 together. It brought in a lot of people from around the city and the whole area of planning. Henry did find that common denominator for everyone, and that was economic development.

It didn't make any difference if you lived on the North Side or the West Side, whether you were a developer. It didn't make any difference what you were, the idea that a "rising tide raises all ships" was one that sold. And that was a marvelous time. A whole lot of things, after that, occur to me that were generated and that Target '90 gave people an opportunity to express some areas of things that were important to the city.

One of the tough things, though, that occurred, I guess in the early parts of the Cisneros term, was the crisis for the financial community—when the real estate people and banking and everything happened here in our state. The '80s were, to me, more of a depression, it wasn't just a recession. Our energy and momentum and things to build and to create came a lot from the real estate and the developer community, and we lost a lot of that in that period.

Events other than HemisFair and Cisneros that have changed San Antonio? UTSA, the downtown River Walk extension. When you think about the Spurs, that team certainly has spread the recognition of San Antonio far and wide. The Medical Center. My father was not supportive of the medical school going out on Fredericksburg Road where it is. He felt that it would take away from the synergism that would come with the Green and the Baptist hospitals and what was invested there. It was an integration of a county hospital that would better serve the constituents by being in that area, rather than moving out so far. And I guess I would have to say that as you would add it up today, he was wrong. He was wrong about some parts of it and right about others.

The issue was that there was not space to grow and to do the things in the urban renewal in the area over time and to create the space that is making possible the Medical School we have there now, with the numbers of hospitals. It just could not have happened. I think about just the traffic, and all the people, and what it would have meant in terms of traffic patterns to move those people into that community.

Nowhere can you escape what the military has been to San Antonio, when you think of United Way and their participation in that, in the functions of the city, when you talk about the parades, all of the things they do. Those has been a really a collaboration with military medicine. Look at the trauma centers, from Wilford Hall and Brooke Army Medical Center being able to support the city. What other community has it? You've got one in the Air Force and one in the Army, and they're right here.

USAA is really, to me, our first huge, major employer that's put the resources and investments in San Antonio. I don't know of anybody that's done as much as USAA has done, if you wanted to go back over time, not only in their volunteers but in their attitude toward United Way and participation in economic development. The conflict with Oscar Wyatt having to do with our City Public Service, and the gas contracts that ultimately resulted in Valero Energy, here in San Antonio, another headquarters. And you get Southwestern Bell here, moving its headquarters from St. Louis.

A More Broadly Based City

All of a sudden San Antonio has moved from the area of being sort of a little big town where you only had a very small number of people in a position to do things with the city to where it's really much more broad than what it used to be. You've got a different community of people with education, with experiences all over the United States and worldwide, with expertise, with reputations, who have moved into San Antonio and created and broadened what was a narrow group of people.

There's been more participation by Hispanics and blacks or minorities, more political than economic. There's been a greater willingness to broaden one's close base of friends, to extend that. And the more venues that you have, the more activities, the more opportunity there is for more people, the more people are involved.

San Antonio used to be a net exporter. When people finished college, they didn't come back to San Antonio. They headed to Dallas, they headed to Houston. That's not the situation today. There are jobs here; there are jobs being created and there are people who come to San Antonio. What a change that was from what it was about HemisFair time.

3. The River Walk and King William District Legacies

Selection of the downtown site for HemisFair was influenced by the location of the River Walk. The two-mile section of the San Antonio River, was landscaped as a park by the city in 1914 and redesigned in 1939–41, in a Works Progress Administration project following the plans of architect Robert H. H. Hugman.

By 1968, however, the River Walk had still attracted little pedestrian or commercial activity. Then a new rush of pedestrian traffic from two riverside hotels built for the fair—the Hilton Palacio del Rio and La Mansion del Rio—sparked the River Walk's modern development into a world-renowned linear park. An extension of the River Walk into HemisFair grounds in 1968 has since been extended twice, once to provide an entry for the three-story River Center Mall and again into an expanded Convention Center.

At the same time, individual restoration was beginning in the nearby King William Street neighborhood, which in 1968 became the first zoned historic district in Texas.

David J. Straus: *Making the River Walk Successful*

David J. Straus is chairman of Straus-Frank Co.

I was at a party in 1959—I don't remember who gave it or where it was—but I remember Walter Corrigan was there. Walter was president of the Chamber of Commerce at the time. A bunch of us were sitting around in a bull session. At that time the River Walk was off limits to the military; it was trashy, full of winos and no one would go down there. And so the subject of Casa Rio came up and they said, "Boy, it'd be nice if we could have a bunch of things like that. Why doesn't someone do something?"

And so I got to thinking about it that night. The next morning I went down and called on Walter Corrigan at the chamber office and said, "Walter, do you remember the conversation last night about the River Walk and

Construction of the Hilton Palacio del Rio beside the San Antonio River for HemisFair helped generate enough river-level pedestrian traffic to make River Walk businesses viable. The River Walk extension into HemisFair grounds begins under the bridge at left.

why doesn't somebody do something about it? Why don't you appoint me as chairman of a committee? Let me develop a committee, mostly people that opened their big mouths at that bull session, and let's see if under the auspices of the chamber we can't do something."

And so he said, "OK, you're chairman of the new committee."

I started recruiting people, and the chamber assigned Harold Robbins to my committee as my staff member. The first thing we did was take an inventory of the Horseshoe Bend. Harold went down to the courthouse and got the deed records identifying who the owners were. Then we started meeting with the owners. And it was pretty futile—I mean, none of them were interested in doing any-thing with their properties, other than what-ever purpose they were being used for at the time.

Then we started looking for pioneers who would invest or who would operate something. I remember talking to Marshall Steves and Nick Catalani, Jim Cullum Sr. I'm trying to think of some of the early ones we got to do some things down there— Heinie Mueller. He's the one, the Little Rhein Steakhouse, he did it; the guy who owns it now bought it from him.

Businessman David Straus.

Anyhow, we started trying to find people who would be prospective tenants so that we could go to the prop-erty owners and say, "We've got somebody who will rent your building if you fix it up." So very slowly we started meeting with every civic club and anybody who would listen to us. This was between 1959 and, I'd say, 1961, and we just couldn't get anybody to do anything.

So Harold and I went to Carmel, California, and to New Orleans. Carmel has very good controls over the development of the town. They have sign ordinances and architectural restrictions and all that and have done a terrific job of keeping the atmosphere of the town intact. Then we went over to New Orleans and met with the Vieux Carre Commission to see what they were doing. We envisioned our development as somewhat similar to the French Quarter.

I sat up all one night with the ordinances from Carmel and New Or-leans and drafted a proposal for City Council to establish the River Walk Commission. I took it to Mayor Walter McAllister and told him what we

As business on the River Walk blossomed with HemisFair, this new retail complex featured Kangaroo Court and Stockman restaurants and La Sirena, a folk art shop.

had in mind. He took it to City Council and that's how the River Walk Commission was established. It was advisory to the Department of Building Permits, whatever they call it. But in actuality, they did have authority because that department wouldn't issue building permits unless the River Walk Commission approved. By the way, I served on the River Walk Commission for 30 years, from 1962, when it was formed, until 1992, when it was consolidated with the other commissions, which I think was a mistake.

Anyhow, gradually we got things going down there, one after another. I bought three buildings. We had so much trouble getting things going that I got a group of investors—three different groups of investors—and we bought three properties, one of them was where Kangaroo Court is now. That's how Hap Veltman got involved. Hap's father, Arthur Veltman Sr., and my father were good friends. In fact, we met in this office—this was my dad's office at the time—and the River Walk was taking more and more of my time. I had a full-time job here.

Mr. Veltman happened to be in here, visiting with my dad, and I said, "Boy, I wish I had somebody to help me." And he said, "Well, why don't you use my son?" I said, "You know, I have never met him. Where is he?" He said, "He's at law school out at St. Mary's University." And so I met with Hap and told him what I was trying to do, and Hap signed on as my unpaid assistant.

In fact, he and I made a bunch of trips down to the Valley. There was a lady who owned the building the Kangaroo Court's in who lived in Weslaco. We went down there a number of times and met with her, and finally talked her into selling that building. I guess my getting these investors together and doing a few buildings to show what we had in mind was probably the principal catalyst in getting other property owners to do something.

I got Jim Hayne involved in getting the Jim Cullum Happy Jazz Band into the Nix Hospital basement, kind of like I got Hap involved. Jim was the one who really got that thing going. I got Marshall Steves involved, and he bought the building that Rio Rio is in now. He got his wife, Patsy, my wife—Louise at the time—and Pat McAlpin. The three gals got with Bob Winn and put in La Sirena. And Marshall bought that building. That was one of the early ones. Then Tita McCamish and a couple of her lady friends put in the Three Wives Antique Shop—where the Hilton is now—with Nick Catalani, who owned the property. They were the early ones.

There was a lady who put in an Italian restaurant. She was the one who caused us to enact the sign ordinance. The first thing she did was open a little Italian restaurant and put a great big flashing red neon sign that said "Pizza" on the River Walk. And, boy, that got us all excited. So we went to the City Council and got it to enact a sign ordinance—which is still in existence—and then we went to her. And, of course, she had "grandfather's rights." She could have kept the sign if she wanted to, but we talked her into taking it down. Early on there were a lot of things like that.

By the time of HemisFair, the River Walk Commission was going. That was probably the busiest time, except probably right now, in the development of things along the River Walk—HemisFair, immediately before and right after HemisFair.

What has made the River Walk work so well? I think the atmosphere. Because of the scale of the river and the walks and arched bridges and

The HemisFair–inspired boom in convention business and River Walk activities led in 1988 to the opening of River Center Mall, on a second River Walk extension. Adjacent to the mall rose the Marriott River Center Hotel, at 42 stories the city's new tallest building.

things like that. The big cypress trees, first of all, establish an atmosphere that's unique. Secondly, I think the people in San Antonio—probably because of the influence of organizations like the Conservation Society—and the historic nature of San Antonio—the Alamo being close by and all that—have created not only an interest but a pride in the River Walk and the area. I think all of those together created some kind of esprit.

Talking about the Paseo del Rio Association, Jimmy Gause came to work at the chamber and was assigned to my committee, along with Harold Robbins.

After the thing started picking up and we needed more people, Jimmy and I went over and called on Charlie Kilpatrick at the Express-News, and said, "We want to establish an association—Paseo del Rio Association—so that we can get some cohesion down there. We would like to have a daily or a weekly column in the newspaper on 'Rio Ramblings.' Charlie accepted and it added to the momentum.

After three extensions into the HemisFair area, how many times can the river successfully be extended without overextending it? Well, in the last thirty days I've had a number of calls from people who are concerned about the overdevelopment of the River Walk. I had one yesterday from Marion Klinger, who used to be on the River Walk Commission with me. I've had several others.

I wrote [Mayor] Nelson Wolff and urged him to reestablish the River Walk Commission, because I thought we needed some more attention. I've written [Mayor] Bill Thornton a couple of times on the same subject. And I think it is a danger that it's getting so crowded down there.

You know, the walks are only about six feet wide and the South Bank has about six or eight bars and restaurants in it clustered very closely together. How do you control something like that? I don't know.

Bill Lyons: *Preserving the Spirit*

Bill Lyons operates the family's Casa Rio Restaurant on the River Walk.

When I was seven years old in 1946, our family's new Casa Rio was the only restaurant on the River Walk. The first week of testing food I got so tired of Mexican food I never thought I wanted to eat it again. We went down every night after the cooks had been cooking and sampled, for a straight week, every evening to try to develop the taste that my grandfather wanted.

Until around HemisFair, my grandfather starved to death most of the time, because people were afraid to go on to the River Walk because of security reasons. The River Walk was off-limits to military personnel in the early years, and there was just not much interest because there were no businesses thriving on the River Walk. So it was just kind of a dead place. But 1968 was the milestone that really turned many people's heads to see a potential benefit in further developing the River Walk.

Has the success since HemisFair caused the River Walk to be overdeveloped? Well, that's a question you'd rather ask than, is it underdeveloped? And that remains to be seen.

I think if we can maintain some of the ambience that has been there in the past and continue to be sensitive to those people who have traditionally used the River Walk, then I think we're in a "plus/plus." The River Walk can still handle more people, even though it gets awfully crowded on some Saturday nights.

Our family also owned and operated the boats on the river for 45 years. I'm not sure when they actually took over the boats. But it had not been a prosperous endeavor as they thought it would be after the river was WPA'd back in the '30s. They thought the river was going to take off, but it didn't take off.

I know Jack White, who had been mayor, ran the boat operation, but the best that I that I can get from our family is that my grandfather said, "I'd like to do the boats to enhance the restaurant operation." And they said, "Well, just take it." He started operating the boats with no payment to the city and was just given the few canoes. I believe he put the first paddleboats on the river.

River Walk restaurateur Bill Lyons.

Somehow HemisFair was the magic for downtown. That started a more positive attitude about what the downtown and the River Walk could become. Personally, I try to cling to what brought us this far and to try to not lose sight of what San Antonio has represented to those who flocked here. So I keep trying to look back and say, "What made the River Walk popular? Why is downtown a nice, comfortable place to be? As we grow and progress, let's try to make sure we don't lose what brought us to the party."

So, since the post-HemisFair success of the River Walk, we've turned down three offers to buy our buildings for a hotel. There is a difficulty when people come to the River Walk as new operators and do not understand what we have tried to develop along the River Walk.

We say, "Someone has got to continue to cling to what makes San Antonio unique." And evidently old, half-falling-down structures have been a part of that uniqueness, and we're going to do our part to maintain it. Schilo's, our other restaurant next door, actually sits on a cedar post foundation.

Those old buildings are tremendously hard to keep up to codes—fire codes, health codes, ADA codes. But there's a certain character and charm that when you lose it, it's gone forever.

James L. Hayne: *Happy Jazz*

James L. Hayne is chairman of Catto & Catto Insurance, with offices in the River Walk's Chandler Building.

I've been in San Antonio since 1961, moved down here with my wife of two years, Roxanna, known as Roxie. I'd been in a band at Williams College called the Spring Street Stompers, all students, except for the clarinet player.

Here in San Antonio I got to a party at the Argyle one night and saw Jim Cullum Sr. and his son Jim Jr., who at that time knew four or five songs in all, playing a little gig, and they didn't have a trombone. So I said, "Say, do you need a trombone? I'll be right back."

I went home, found that thing, came back, oiled it, put some water on it, got the slide working, and sat in with them. It was a six-piece

Jazz aficionado James Hayne.

band. Jim Cullum Sr. couldn't get over it. That started our relationship.

A couple of us were interested in opening up a jazz joint. There was a very talented fellow in San Antonio, long since moved to Dallas, named Frank Blaybaum. He sang with the Barbershop Chorus here, and he was a talented arranger, loved the music, loved jazz, had heard Cullum. One day we were walking up and down the river; you remember in those days the only thing there was Casa Rio? We found this kind of abandoned basement under the Nix Hospital, actually under the Nix parking garage. And we said, "Wouldn't it be fun if . . . ?"

So, I took it from there—Frank was otherwise busy—and put together 22 of my friends and acquaintances and asked them for $500 to $1,000 each to open up the place we came up with named The Landing. Half of them thought it was a great idea, the other half were humoring me.

It started in April of 1963. David Brooks, who was then CEO of the Nix Hospital, was an enthusiastic participant. Herb Kelleher, who is now CEO of Southwest Airlines, donated his legal time to put together the corporation that owned The Landing, Inc. Then we had Arthur and Frates Seeligson and Buzz Butler, Johnny Matthews and Ed Muir. Those were the pre-mixed-drink days. People brought their bottles and bought setups, they "brown-bagged" it.

Of course, I had to make that deal with Jim Senior. I kept asking him to do this. He said he'd already had his own club in Dallas, it didn't work and he didn't want any part of it. Of course he was dying to do it, but at the time he was running that Cullum whole-sale food business. And so, he finally gave in. He said, "All right, man, but only if you play trombone." So that's why I had to start playing there with the original group.

Jim Cullum Jr. built his father's pioneering River Walk jazz band into one featured weekly on National Public Radio's "Live from the Landing."

With the boom in business along the River Walk that came with HemisFair, about 1975 the Happy Jazz Band went from talented amateurs to a professional band when Jim Cullum Sr. and Jr. started another corporation called Happy Jazz. We gave them our blessing.

I suppose they could have bought us out, but, on the other hand, they couldn't afford to. And, going from having daytime jobs, Jim Jr., who's kept this going for all these years, especially needed all the support he could get. So we all welcomed his taking hold of it and doing his own thing.

Well, he's turned out to be a pretty good business manager, too. I mean, how else could he, as tough as that go is, play the original classic jazz every evening on the river and, incidentally, do extensive traveling around the United States and the world playing this music, and on National Public Radio, too, and create a lasting historical resource on jazz?

As the River Walk got more hotels, more tourists, more conventions, Jim did better. And in fact, in some years he prospered, relatively speaking, or at least relative to the other years. The band reflects the evolution of the River Walk.

Walter N. Mathis: *Reviving a Downtown Neighborhood*

Investor Walter Mathis is the pioneering force in the restoration of the King William Historic District on the southwestern edge of downtown.

My house south of Olmos Park was a very nice cottage on Mulberry and Stadium Drive. I went to a rally in the Sunken Gardens Theater opposing a proposed expressway, and Wanda Ford had this huge map up there. I looked and they had the route through all the green areas. There was a tiny pear-shaped object in the middle of the right lane, and I said, "Oh, my God, that's my swimming pool!" And the McAllister Freeway went right through my house.

I was very much opposed to it, but didn't do any active fighting of it. Mayor McAllister, who was such a great guy, came to see me and said, "Now, Walter, don't be active in this anti-freeway thing; you're going to come out just all right." I didn't want to lose my home, but I had to.

Beginning at the time of HemisFair, Walter Mathis helped revive a historic downtown neighborhood.

So I started looking around. Since childhood I've known about the King William District, because many of the old families still live down here. But I rode around, and I saw this old house that was the Ike Pryor house. It fascinated me because of the number of windows on the south side. I made some inquiries, and found it had been divided into about eight apartment units. The porches had been closed, and the entire backyard was a big gravel parking area. It was in terrible disrepair. I made an attempt to find the owner, which I did; he lived out of state. After much negotiation I bought the house, at 401 King William Street.

And I was greatly encouraged by O'Neil Ford—the architect and Wanda's husband. He knew all about the house and about the construction. And the reason that it fascinated him was the construction, the stone construction. It's just made of thousands of huge limestone blocks. The four-story quality of it appealed to me. That was during HemisFair, in 1968.

I had to get out of my old house, so I moved to a downtown hotel and started construction here. I got a superb carpenter named Basilio Gonzalez, and he had 14 employees. They went to work on this house. What moldings and all were gone, they found pieces of and reproduced. They worked a year and half restoring this house. Completely gutted the house. I did it with new copper plumbing from the street in, and hundreds of loads of plaster had to go out. And put all new plumbing facilities in, and restored the rooms the way they were. The house had 15 stained-glass windows that were taken out; luckily I found them in a pile in the basement.

O'Neil Ford was involved in the project, but he didn't charge me a penny. I called his secretary once and I said, "Look, Mr. Ford's been over here three times this week, and he's got to send me a bill." She said, "Oh, no, he'd never send you a bill. He's so pleased you're doing the house over." We got help from all sorts of places. The Sherwin-Williams Co. sent some of their research people down here, and we took samples of the plaster and found the original paint colors. I renamed it Villa Finale because it's going to be my last home. I'll never have another house.

My friends were saying, "Why are you redoing a house in that decaying area of town?" Crazy. I brought a good friend of mine who's a lawyer over after I bought the house. "Walter," he said, "you haven't signed anything yet, I hope." My brother, who was an architect, looked it all over, because the neighborhood was so bad, and he said, "Well, I'll tell you this, Walter, it can't do anything but get better, it's so bad."

After that, I tried to help improve the neighborhood. I bought 14 additional houses in the district and started restoring them. After my house was finished, I moved these crews into these other places. I would buy one of these big, fine old houses and then I would fix the foundation and put a new tin roof on it. Then I would attempt to sell the house to either someone I knew or someone I didn't know, who would use their money to restore it.

I did many deals with nothing down. I carried the paper and enabled them, particularly young couples, to spend their money to remodel. But they had to agree to restore the house properly. About that time, the city established the Historic Preservation Ordinance and established the Historic Review Board, so all plans and architectural changes had to be cleared.

How long did it take to get the other 14 houses restored and occupied? Oh, that happened over a period of, say, ten years. But then it got out of my hands, which is wonderful, because other people started buying houses and restoring them. I couldn't do the whole thing, but I did get 14 of them going. Now almost the entire district has been redone. There are still some holdouts. It's not quite as desirable as you'd like it to be.

King William Street's Norton-Polk-Mathis House is in view of the HemisFair Tower.

Lately, there's been another effect, the business revival on South Alamo called Southtown. And the bed and breakfasts. I personally am not opposed to bed and breakfasts, because not many people really want a house of the size of some of these houses because of the utility bills and so on. Some of the neighbors down here are very much opposed to bed and breakfasts, but as long as they're handled properly I think it's all right. I think there are around 30—I'm not sure. I restored a house called the "Oge House" on Washington Street, where General Oge lived. He was the commander of the Arsenal. I sold it to some people from California, and they made a very fine bed and breakfast out of it, the big, three-story house up off of the King William Park.

The Conservation Society came into King William and restored the Wulff House shortly after that. O'Neil and Wanda Ford and I were really instrumental in getting them to do that. The house was for sale, and it was going to be a mortuary. A lot of us who lived here just thought it would ruin our street to have that, so we went to the Conservation Society and asked if

SAN ANTONIO
CONSERVATION SOCIETY

they would accept it if we got it. We got a committee, I contacted 150 people and then we had a number of very generous people. Mrs. Irene Sheerin's family gave a matching grant of a $150,000, and we raised $300,000 and bought the property. The Conservation Society got a federal grant, and we saved the Wulff House. We were very proud of that effort. It's the Conservation Society headquarters now, but it's the keynote for the whole district.

Prior to that, Mrs. Edna Steves Vaughan had given the Steves House to the Conservation Society. I felt that my house, in between, would kind of link it all together.

Gentrification hasn't really happened here, because many of the original families have kept their old houses. Gentrification means moving out the original settlers and moving new people in, and that really hasn't happened here.

4. The Political Legacy

Heroic efforts of San Antonio's old-line business and political establishment may have achieved HemisFair '68, but the fair, ironically, is often seen as the Old Guard's last hurrah. Political forces unleashed by the fair led to replacement of the old order with a more democratic, egalitarian political scene, portrayed here by five former mayors of the city.

Charles Becker: *Smiting the Old Guard*

Charles Becker, then chairman of Handy-Andy Supermarkets, was first elected to San Antonio's City Council in 1971 and served as mayor from 1973 to 1975.

When we came here the first place we lived was on West Park, between Main Avenue and San Pedro. That was considered to be almost the extent of the North Side of San Antonio. I remember very well that every night during the summertime all of us kids in the neighborhood would play under the streetlights, and our parents would generally call us in at 9 or 10 o'clock in the evening. I compare that with what I know of San Antonio today. I don't advise anybody to play under the street lights today.

The city was probably 125,000 people in those days. It was an extremely friendly environment and, for the most part, people who were doing things all knew each other, I wouldn't say intimately, but at least very well, because there wasn't that big a complex of business and industry in those days, and there wasn't the hustle-bustle.

My father was the type who had a great sense of dedication and duty, and felt that if the community had treated you well and you were prospering that you should give something back of your self, of your time and your effort. So I'd always thought, someday when I had the ability I'd give some of my time away from my business, which I took over after his demise.

I remember very well that two members of the Good Government League came out and visited me about running for the council in 1971. I told them I would be happy to do so, with the one stipulation that we open all of the board meetings of the city-owned agencies and municipal-owned functions—such as the City Public Service, City Water Board, Transit Authority, which is now VIA—to the public so we could see how their city functions were being operated. We all agreed on that, and two GGL people and myself and one other gentleman who was there as a visitor shook hands on it. I thought that was all that was necessary, a handshake.

In the reform period following HemisFair, mayoral candidate Charles Becker defeated the candidate of the long-entrenched Good Government League.

So we ran for public office, and in those days the GGL always won, with the exception of Pete Torres and Dr. Ford Neilsen. I waited for 30 or 45 days and I asked the mayor, Jack Gatti, "Well, when are we going to open those meetings up to the public?" He said, "I've been meaning to talk to you about that. I've been thinking about that and I've changed my mind." I said, "Well, we shook hands on it." He said, "Well, that's too bad."

I said, "Well, Jack, we shook hands on it and that's all that I remember about the transaction, and that should be good enough. I'm going to open it up anyway." He said, "You can't do that; you're not a member of those boards." I said, "Well, we'll see who can do it."

And sure enough Al Padillo, Gilbert Garza, Leo Mendoza—I forget one or two other bomb-throwers on the council—and myself did just that. We opened the meetings up to the public. And we started one hell of a war, I'll tell you. We were all GGL council members, but they were quasi, if you will, GGL council.

It was about that time that the Hispanics in this town, I think after watching the machinations of Pete Torres, began to feel that they should come forward and do something for their segment of the community.

The facts of the matter are that I created such havoc down there. Here I was supposed to be an establishment person, and in a sense of the word I was, I mean I represented probably one of the biggest private business employers in the city. But when we shook hands on opening the meetings up, I took that seriously.

And after that I wasn't trustworthy, you know. I wasn't fit to wear the GGL membership badge any longer. I was a double-crosser, or a trouble-maker, or a maverick or whatever the hell. And so when it came time to run again, they kept stringing me along and stringing me along and I knew the game they were playing, of course. They waited, and finally agreed that I could run in Place 3, which is where I ran the first time; we ran in places in those days, in that at-large thing. They got Roy Barrera Sr., the attorney, to run against me.

Roy and I had three meetings. I said, "Roy, as long as you don't run head on against me, I'll help you get elected. If you want to be mayor, I'll help you get elected. I'll go on the North Side, up and down Loop 410 and to luncheon clubs, introduce you as the mayoral candidate, and everything else; just don't run in my place! 'Cause if you do we're going to have a hell of a fight!" That was when the council elected the mayor.

He said, "All right." We shook hands on it. One night three times, a Monday night. The following Thursday of that same week, it came out in the newspaper that Roy Barrerra was going to make a mayor's race out of it and run against Becker in Place 3. Well, that of course started World War III. I wasn't about to back down. Anyway, we ran, and of course I beat him. Then five members of the group that was elected voted to make me mayor.

Opening City Public Service

But there were some comical aspects of the thing that are really tragic when you stop and think about it. The City Public Service, for example, used to have meetings on the third or fourth floor, in oak-paneled offices, a gorgeous layout. When we opened it up to the public they moved up on the very top floor. There was an unfinished concrete floor, and the bar joist were still exposed, no air conditioning.

It was like a sauna in there in the summer. I was concerned about Jack Locke Sr. because he was 80. Finally, I said, "Listen, you'd better do something about Mr. Locke, because I'm afraid he's going to expire up here one of these days." They were kind enough to get some plyboard and create a boxlike affair and put in two window units, one at each end, and that was an enclosure of a sort. And we all got in there in that thing.

But those were public affairs, and those things belong to the people. The public's entitled to know how their affairs are being handled, because if they are not handled properly, it just adds to the cost of kilowatt hours or cubic feet of water or gallons or whatever the world measurements you're using.

When I was on the City Public Service Board as mayor, they were talking about building a coal-fired energy plant. I was trying to bring into play the practice of open bidding, competitive bidding. Well, of course I ran aground on it; I was always outvoted on that, but the thing boiled down to where I was told what the whole thing, every nut, bolt and screw, turn-key, was going to cost. They had two bidders already, one for $26 million, one for $50-some-odd million.

I said, "Who are the bidders?" "Well, we can't tell you that." I said, "All right then, who is the lowest bid?" "Well, we can't tell you that." I said, "OK."

You know what it finally cost? It was in the paper one day about seven or eight years after they opened it. And in that little bitty type way in the back, they admitted it had cost over $250-some-odd million. It'll build you a bridge from here to the moon, if you'll give me a cost-plus contract with the United States government or someone that can pay the bills.

We had a printout once a month of everything the City Public Service ever bought for that preceding month: rolled-coiled copper wire of all gauges, and God knows, wrapped and unwrapped, and you know, they buy a myriad of things over there, just an astronomical amount of stuff. It's a huge operation.

The printout was one of these IBM things that folds, there'd maybe be five or six items to the page. There were always four bidders to each item. Once down that page, you'd turn to the next page, the same thing, next page, and each of those composite parts would have identical prices. All four suppliers, the same identical amount, page after page after page, whether it was those insulators up on the telephone poles or whether it was poles or whether it was bits and augers.

I brought it up a couple of times, and no one could see that there was anything unusual about that. Well, of course, in the first place it's a mathematical impossibility to ever have figures come out that way.

So I was mayor, an ex-officio member of the board, but they couldn't tell me who bid what to build that power plant? They didn't want to. See, I'd lost their confidence by then. I was a troublemaker. Had we not shaken hands on it, it would have been an entirely different matter.

Now we've gone to single-member districts, we have term limits— two two-year terms, and 11 members rather than 9. We tried to bring about a compromise toward the latter part of my tenure of office. Four would run at-large, North, East, South and West, cut the city up in equal quadrants. Hildebrand, east and west. San Pedro, north and south; then have probably five or six others run in districts within those quadrants to get a flavor of both districting and at-large.

I hadn't been in office when I was the mayor two or three weeks at the very most, when COPS, or Communities Organized for Public Service, made its first appearance before the City Council. They were talking about how they had to walk through water that was standing that deep after rains, how the kids were getting mosquito bites and those would develop into impetigo and the unfairness of it all.

Sam Granata was the city manager, and I asked, "Sam, how long have they been promising these people restitution or relief, if you will, from these conditions? I know you can't fix it all at once, it'd probably take a couple of billion dollars to fix it all at once." But I said, "How long have they been promised?"

He said, "I've been here 20-some odd years and they've been promised every year that I've been here." I said, "Well, we're going to do something about it." And, by God, we passed a five point-something million dollar bond issue right then and there. Didn't take us five minutes to do it.

And then I said, and council agreed with all of this, "You find out through your department heads the most seriously needed things on the West Side of San Antonio, and work some of these inequities on drainage and flooding and sewage and all that kind of stuff. In about three months they came back to us with their recommendations and we passed another $47 million just like that. Those bonds went to market and they were sold immediately.

That's the beginning of the COPS organization, because they came down and they hit a home run. I didn't do it for favor. I didn't do it for public aggrandizement or anything. I did it because I thought it was the only fair thing.

On single-member districts, I think there's been some ward-heeling, but I think there's always going to be some ward-heeling. That's just a part of politics, you know. I think that, all things being equal, and looking at it with hindsight and everything, I think there's been some abuse. But, all things considered, I would say it's been pretty well handled.

Now term limitation helps bring that about. That's the watchdog that sort of takes care of people who want to roost down there. If I can learn how things work in not a great period of time I think anybody can. It's really not that difficult; it requires tremendous patience and sacrifice and all that to go to all these meetings and sit there forever and a day and all. But if you have any type of adult mind whatsoever in your possession, I think the average guy can ferret out what's real and what isn't.

Since HemisFair there's been progress on ethnic relations and more job opportunities, there's no question about that. To the best of my recollection, when I was at City Hall I don't recall one single Hispanic or black department head. They were almost all Anglo. There were some assistants who might have been Hispanic, but a department head? There just weren't any. Today if you go over there I'd say it's probably 80 percent Hispanic and black and 20 percent Anglo.

I don't think the pendulum's swung too far. It's an opportunity, and if people are willing to apply themselves and work hard there's no reason in the world why the color of their skin or their ethnic background should have a thing to do with their job opportunities or anything like that.

As long as, of course, they're not troublemakers like me.

Lila Cockrell: *Political Transition*

Lila Cockrell was a city council member from 1963 to 1970 and served as mayor from 1975 to 1981 and again from 1989 to 1991.

I lived in San Antonio as a very young child, but then, when my father died when I was just 1 1/2, my mother and I did not return until 1956, when my husband, Sid Cockrell Jr., accepted the position of executive director of the Bexar County Medical Society. We moved with our two young girls from Dallas and established our home in San Antonio.

I was first aware of a very attractive city. I especially loved the river. One of my first memories is having a lunch on the river with my uncle, C.

Lila Cockrell was first elected mayor in 1975.

Stanley Banks, and thinking that this is a beautiful and romantic city. In 1951 San Antonio adopted the council/manager form of government. At that time, the Good Government League was getting under way; I think it came into existence in about 1955 as a reform movement to try to have a clean, honest, honorable city government with a businesslike approach to managing the affairs of the city.

I had served two terms as president of the San Antonio League of Women Voters. In January or February of 1963, I had a call from Mayor Walter McAllister, who said some people would like to come out and talk to me. When they came out, they arrived in two cars. About four or five gentlemen got out of each car and all headed for my door. Their mission was to ask me to be the first woman candidate to run on the GGL ticket for City Council. They really did not ask me many questions; they just talked about city government and about why they had felt that I could make a contribution.

I asked them just one question: "If I agree to be a candidate, will you ever be coming to me at a future time to try and tell me how I am supposed to vote, or is my vote going to be my own?" And they pledged that they would never in any way try to tell me how I was to vote, but that the invited candidates would exercise good judgment. I told them I would have to talk it over with my husband and family and let them know. And after Sid and I talked it over, we decided that it would be OK to go ahead, and so I did.

The council served more as a board of directors in those times. I recall our meetings were not too long, maybe a couple of hours. And we occasionally had a citizen to be heard, usually, say, from the Chamber of Commerce discussing some city issue. There was not a lot of controversy. We had our informal "B" sessions, they used to call them "bat roost" sessions. We would have a bowl of chili in the basement conference room and talk about what was coming up in the future, and make plans for when things would be on the formal council agenda. It was not very controversial.

One of the issues 30 years ago was water. Doesn't that sound familiar? I believe as long as I've been in San Antonio that water has been on the list of issues that needed to be resolved. But other than that, when I came on in 1963 the city was just gearing up for HemisFair '68. It was five years in the future, but there were a lot of things that the city government itself had to do. We had to get a bond issue passed to build a convention center. I look back and think of the cost at that time of the San Antonio Convention Center. We had passed a $30 million bond issue. It was just amazing how many things were in that bond issue. The entire complex could be built, I think, for about $12 or $13 million.

There were issues looming, however, that were controversial. I know there were discussions about public housing, which was controversial. As we went into the mid- and later '60s, there were discussions about whether it would or would not be advisable for us to try to be one of the model cities in Lyndon Johnson's Model Cities Program. I was pushing very heavily for it, and we did get the necessary votes on the council to be a part of that program. With Congressman Henry B. Gonzalez's help, we were one of the first five cities that were named to be a Model City.

I was elected first in 1963, reelected in '65, '67 and '69, and in '69 I was mayor pro-tem. I resigned in about 1970 because I was nearing the end of my term and my mother had invited me to make a very special trip with her to Europe. I knew it was about time for me to be stepping off anyway, so I went ahead and quit a little bit early.

I assumed that was going to be the end of my political career and took a job. I was very surprised to be approached again in about the fall of '72 by the GGL and asked to consider becoming a candidate, again, for City Council. I thought about it and really had a little bit of mixed feelings as to whether I should consider going back. But I said yes. And I was elected again in '73.

The Beginning of Change

That was the beginning, though, of change. That was the year when Charles Becker was elected mayor, and the Good Government League had come to a point where the young folks who had started the GGL back in the mid-'50s and who came in as the reform movement had perhaps become more complacent. I felt, personally, that they were beginning to be out of touch with the fact that so many sectors of our community, who had previously felt under-represented, were wanting to have more and more of a voice.

At any rate, in that particular campaign five GGL members were elected and four non-GGL candidates were elected, including Charles Becker. The GGL put their designated mayoral candidate up against Charles Becker. That was a very ugly campaign, quite frankly. After that campaign, which Charles Becker won, and he won as a council member, there was confusion because of the GGL candidate for mayor who had been defeated. I nominated Dr. Jose San Martin as someone who had run with me on the GGL ticket and whom I nominated for mayor. But Charles Becker was elected by a 5-4 majority.

That was the last time the mayor was elected by the council, because in the fall of '74 there was an amendment passed to the City Charter for direct election of the mayor by the people. I was designated as the candidate for mayor on the Good Government League ticket in '75. However, just three of us from that ticket were elected, because the Good Government League had begun to slip strongly. The other two persons who were elected were Henry Cisneros and Phil Pyndus.

There were six members elected from what was called the Independent Team. I recall there was some speculation that I was going to be mayor in name only, and that the real power would reside in the six. I approached that challenge from the point of view that each of us had been elected by the voters and that each of us had a responsibility to work together and to try to do the best for our city. While the so-called party lines were manifested right in the beginning, before very long we were finding that we could work on issues in different alignments. In fact, the Good Government League at that point simply went out of business. And so from then on, everyone who ran just as an independent.

The Advent of Single-Member Districts

In January of '77, another major change was approved by voters. That was the move for single-member districts. It really came about through a challenge by the Department of Justice. The City of San Antonio had proceeded with a number of annexations, and these annexations were being challenged by the Department of Justice under the Voting Rights Act. One option was just to go into an extended, lengthy battle as some of other cities had done. I felt we ought to move on, so the proposition was placed to the voters of endorsing a single-member district plan. It passed fairly narrowly, and we were able to move on with the election and proceed under the new rules.

City government has since changed a great deal. I think in many ways, though, as we have become a larger city, it was something that was absolutely needed. Everything you do has some good points and, obviously, has some weak points. But I felt that at the very least it offered a much more direct opportunity to see that citizens in every part of the city have a voice in city government.

I think we have avoided some of the worst examples of ward-heeling, where council members lose sight of overall problems of the city. When I became mayor again in '77, I was faced with a City Council that was almost all brand new. We had seven new members, and only four of us were holdovers. Each had been elected from his or her district with a mandate of "go down there and bring fresh blood, fresh ideas, new ideas to City Council, get it all straightened out."

That meant that we had a lot of energy, for one thing, but a lot of energy challenging anything that might be regarded as the status quo. And so, ideas that had been previously tried and rejected had to be tried again. The advice given to us by city staff members, in many cases, was suspect to some of these new members.

It was not an easy two years. But I think during those two years we had a learning experience going on. The new council members were learning a lot more about city government than they were aware of before. The incumbent members were learning more about the point of view and the concerns of the new persons who were representing these districts. I think before the term was over, we were able to make it work. The trends were the flexing of muscles around the thought that now the council was a council where the majority were minority members and where there appeared to be some effort to divide up votes along ethnic lines or geographical lines, and I felt that we needed to get around that.

We needed to be looking at not only how each district's needs were met but also at how we could all work together on the needs of the whole city. And I think by the end of the term we had more or less gotten past that particular problem.

I served as mayor until 1981. I think by the time that we came to the end of that period we had seen great growth in the ability of all council members now understanding the system, being a part of the system, understanding how you work with the different neighborhoods, the different sectors of the city. I thought it was all very healthy.

I know there was some concern in the business community, particularly in the earlier part of this period, that the council was very argumentative. The meetings were lasting so long, but I felt that it was a healthy thing to have all of these issues laid on the table and looked at very openly, because in the past many of them had been problems that were seething just below the surface.

Then Henry Cisneros was mayor for eight years. In '89 he decided not to run for reelection. I was in his office on a different matter and when he had sort of leaked the word to the media that he was not going to run. The media people were waiting outside his office to ask him more about it, so he turned to me and said, "Are you going to run, Lila?" And I said, "Well, a few people have mentioned it to me." And I said, "I might take a look at it." And I did.

Well, you know, Henry is a very, very talented public official and political person. I think he just loves it. All through that fall, when I would see him take particularly active roles I would think to myself, that really doesn't look like someone who is ready to step out, but maybe he just wants to keep up the momentum to the end of his term. Several times I sort of repeated the question to him, before I went too deep into it. "Are you sure this is what you want to do?" And I was told very definitely, yes, he had made up his mind that was what he was going to do.

Then in January there was the Alamodome campaign. Henry just put himself into that totally. In the beginning it looked as if it was going to be almost impossible to pass. It was his crusade to get the Alamodome passed. When he got through with it and won, it was just a great high for him. I can certainly understand that. I could certainly understand that some of his close friends and associates would say, "Oh, why don't you go on and run for mayor?"

I could see this little movement developing, but Henry still had not mentioned it to me. I was an announced candidate. I had raised funds. Several other potential candidates had withdrawn, based on my candidacy. It was in January before the filing deadline, so I was asked by the media, "Are you going to withdraw if Henry decides to run again?"

I said, "No. I will stand my ground, because, based on his assurance that he was not going to be a candidate, I have now invested six months in preparation, people have made contributions and given support to me and, however it comes out, I'm going to stay in the race." Then Henry, after thinking it over, made an announcement that he felt that it was a matter of honor not to become a candidate. And I won election again.

Henry Cisneros: *Democracy Achieved*

Henry Cisneros was elected to City Council in 1975 and served as mayor from 1981 to 1989. He was U.S. Secretary of Housing and Urban Development under President Bill Clinton, then lived in Los Angeles as head of the Hispanic television network Univision and returned to San Antonio in 2001 to develop housing in low-income neighborhoods.

I was born and raised in San Antonio. Born June 11, 1947, at the Nix Hospital and raised on the West Side, on Monterey Street, went to San Antonio schools, Catholic schools—Little Flower Elementary School, Central Catholic High School. I finished Texas A&M in May of 1968, when HemisFair had just opened. I went to work for the city manager's office. I had an opportunity, thanks to Mayor Walter McAllister, who had visited A&M and I was assigned to host him there, and to Jerry Henckel, who was then the city manager, to serve as an intern in the city manager's office for the summer of 1968.

One of my assignments that summer was to work on some of the problems at HemisFair. There were some practical problems related to security and problems related to the Tower of the Americas and other things. So, I have fond memories of HemisFair, both as a wonderful fair and as very enjoyable. Mary Alice and I were dating at the time, and we attended many HemisFair-related events that summer.

But also there was work. My work at the city involved everything from ongoing problems at HemisFair to consideration of the post-HemisFair use. There was discussion then, already, about how the buildings would be used after the fair closed.

I became interested in city government, urban issues, during my junior year at Texas A&M when I was asked to attend a conference at West Point on contemporary problems. I was one of the delegates from A&M to make that conference. Now this is 1966. The cities had been burning. There had already been riots in Los Angeles and Cleveland. John Lindsey was the mayor of New York, and he was keeping the city from burning by walking the streets of the city with his sleeves rolled up. I always knew I that wanted to be in some kind of public service. I assumed that would be either the military—the Vietnam War was raging—or perhaps the space program.

I wanted to be as productive and helpful to the country as I could, and it occurred to me during this period that could be done by working in the cities. So that was the first decision. I started then to alter my curriculum to take courses that were city-related and government-related, and then econom- ics-related. I was awarded a fellowship to graduate school. It was that summer, after graduation but before going back to graduate school, that I worked in the city of San Antonio.

I was asked to come back while I was in the graduate degree program and be assistant director of the Model Cit- ies Program here, on the West Side of San Antonio. So I had an even deeper grounding then in urban problems, San Antonio style—drainage, flooding, gangs, drugs, schooling.

The Model Cities Program was the effort of that day to try to really turn the West Side around. It left a perma- nent legacy. You can see the flood con- trol projects, streets, sidewalks, new schools, boys' clubs, centers, etc. Then

Henry Cisneros in 1981.

I decided to go east and pursue a graduate degree at George Washington University. Became a White House fellow. Went to Harvard. Did my mili- tary service. And then returned to San Antonio in 1974.

In the fall of 1974, I had been here about four months. Kemper Diehl wrote an article in the *Express-News* listing the challenges of the upcoming city elections the following April, and listing the persons in town, of a younger generation, who might be the kind of young professionals who could join the city government and make a difference. He listed names like William Elizondo, then an optometrist, and myself, and several other people. That was the first idea I had. It sort of picked up steam with my friends, my family, my uncle Ruben Mungia, long on the edge of politics. People began to talk to him about it. And from there came the first suggestion that I should consider it. By the following January, three months later, I was an announced candidate and by April elected to the City Council at age 27.

My uncle, Ruben Munguia, the one urging me to run, was head of a West Side group that was a kind of an adjunct of the Good Government League—West Side Coalition, they called themselves. George de la Garza, former member of City Council; Felix Trevino, former member of the City Council; my Uncle Ruben, who himself had run for county commissioner, a small businessman on the West Side, a printer. They made the recommendation about three Latino candidates and the GGL accepted them.

The Good News Was the GGL Selected the Candidates

It was bad timing, in the sense that the Good Government League was selecting candidates. That's the good news, that you would get selected to run as a young professional. The bad news is that there was a serious alternate ticket, for the first time, that had a new reform tilt to it. As things worked out, the reform group—Independent Team they called themselves—elected six people, and only three GGL people were elected—myself, Lila Cockrell and Phil Pyndus. We were the last of the GGL.

This was the first election, 1975, in which the mayor was elected outright, and Lila Cockrell was elected. She was the GGL standard-bearer, but she ended up with a council of six people who were Independent Team. As fate would have it, they didn't know what they had. That is to say, they ended up abusing their mandate.

The real problem was that they were on the same page with respect to a couple of very difficult issues in the community. Those were kind of the developer-fueled agenda of taking over the water board, fueling the continued developer growth, riding roughshod over the aquifer issue. Even though they were elected as reformers, it was fundamentally a different schism in the community. It was the new money, which they represented, versus the old money, which the GGL represented, and it was just two factions.

Unfortunately, within a few months they had made some decisions—for example to vote for a shopping mall to be located over the aquifer; to name key developers to the water board and other things of that nature. That quickly gained for them a reputation as, basically, tools of the developers. That may sound harsh, but that's the way it broke out.

We also had the natural gas contract at that time. This group ended up positioning themselves in favor of a settlement with Coastal-Lovaca, which was easily drawn in the public's eyes as a connection between Oscar Wyatt and Charles Becker, the godfather of the Independent Team. Well, suffice it to say that by the end of the first term, no one from that Independent Team came back to the council.

And we also have to remember this was the period in which COPS was being formed. COPS came into existence in 1974. This group we are talking about was elected in 1975. By 1976 and 1977, COPS basically called their hand in their developer-oriented North Side utility extension and water policies. And this group that had intended to come in as reformers overplayed their hand, slammed down on COPS on the water issues, slammed down on COPS on the Coastal-Lovaca settlement. And before very long they were seen as, basically, completely blowing the mandate, the opportunity that they had.

In 1976 there was an election on the question of the mall over the aquifer. The public voted it down in massive, massive numbers, not to allow that zoning and to protect the water supply. People like myself were on the right side of that election, campaigning for the community, and the other side was basically positioned on the wrong side. By 1976, the Justice Department declared the San Antonio system of at-large elections to be unconstitutional and required the city to either fight it in court or offer an election to the public.

I can say that the Independent Team's reform instincts did come out in this case. They'd always been reformers about the structure of government. They ended up putting forward a very good plan, that the majority of us voted for, which districted the city into an 11-person council—one mayor, 10 districts. That passed by the equivalent of 10 votes for precinct in the city. It was a very close election: 31,000 to 29,000, as I recall.

I feel today, as strongly as I did then, that the city had been characterized by a pretty dramatic absence of real democracy. The city was run pretty much by an elite— business elite, chamber of commerce elite. There was a genuine sense of inclusion only after the districts went into place. And, in this city with so many problems to resolve, it was really impossible to begin to address those underlying problems until the preliminary question of representation and democracy was first addressed. Only districts did that.

Once that was done we could get on to other serious business, and the record over the last 25 years has not been a bad record. The city has taken substantial leaps forward during this time period. Whether it's the downtown revitalization, or HemisFair, or the dome, or the nuclear project, I think it is not correct to say that no one could take the citywide view, because the record would contradict that. There's been quite a citywide progress.

The First Ethnic Minority Majority

The 1977 election was pretty dramatic in that for the first time, there was a ethnic minority-majority: five Latinos and Joe Webb from the black community and five traditional San Antonians—Anglos. This from a council that had never had more than three minorities, including the council extant at that time; Richard Teniente and myself and Claude Black were the three minorities on that previous council. Now all of a sudden we went to a majority, 6 out of 11, and that majority was not only different in ethnicity but in age and in background. It had an average age of sub-35 among the minorities and an average age of near 60-plus among the traditional group.

So there were vast differences: Rudy Ortiz, who was a social worker; Bennie Eureste was a professor of social work at Our Lady of the Lake; myself, a professor at the University of Texas; Frank Wing, a civil service worker at Kelly Field; Joe Alderete, community activist and political operative; Joe Webb. Everybody under 35 years of age, versus Phil Pyndus, Lila Cockrell, John Steen and Glen Hartmann.

The previous Independent Team was defeated in the process. Richard Teniente was no longer there, defeated by Alderete. Claude Black retired. Bob Billa was beaten by Helen Dutmer. I mean the city was, I think, shocked. And there was a moment of—gasp!—What have we done here?

It was a very rocky first two years, very rocky. We didn't know, frankly, how to use those six votes. The community was constantly expecting more and testing and pushing for more. There were some very tough showdown votes on aquifer matters, where the inclination was to go whole-hog and make changes the legal system wouldn't allow.

The majority wanted to impose a moratorium over all development over the aquifer. It would have been, in effect, reverse condemnation of the land and cost billions of dollars in lawsuits. But it was very, very tough, because we had members then who felt they'd been elected to do the people's will. And I think we all, but some in particular, had a keener sense of what government could do. As if being elected to local government you could change things overnight. It just wasn't to be.

So we had a very tough time in the first term. It ended with a bond issue that the majority of six tried to put forward that was, we felt, balanced for the time toward the poor neighborhoods, but which the five members opposed. Now we had the votes to put it on the ballot, but Mayor Cockrell and Glen Hartmann and others led the push to defeat it at the polls.

In 1979, I was elected by huge margins in my central city district, and Mayor Cockrell was re-elected. I think my margins were 90 percent or so. I contemplated running for mayor in 1979, but really needed quite a lot of spade work with the business community which, because of the tumultuous nature of '77 through '79, I don't think, had confidence that a minority mayor, or, for that matter, I, was ready to do it. By 1981, Mayor Cockrell resigned for personal reasons, largely associated with her husband and his health.

By this point I had some difficulty with some of the positions the minority council group was promoting, and I had broken with them on some key votes, notably the moratorium over the aquifer, on which I abstained. Another key vote was a plan to penalize the H. B. Zachry Co. for some homes that had flaws that they had built in the southeast part of the city. I didn't feel that was the right way to do it and ended up negotiating a different approach, but under great pressure from COPS. I think that the business community had seen that I could, in effect, stand on my own.

When Gen. Robert McDermott created United San Antonio, he asked Raul Jimenez and me to join him in pushing for the business community, for the civic sector and for the political community-public sector. I worked hard at proving to people that I really could take a citywide view, so when Mayor Cockrell decided not to run for reelection I got calls immediately from some of the major figures in the business community, saying that they would support me.

But the schism that had existed in 1975, that new money–old money split, still existed. John Steen, in fact, was the candidate of the old money, and I became the candidate of the new San Antonio, including a lot of the new money. So people like Red McCombs and Cliff Morton, Morris Jaffe, Jim Dement and Dan Parman supported me and were regarded as traitors to their class and their generation by the Steen forces.

Some very good people stepped up to the plate for me, among them those that I mentioned and others. I campaigned on the North Side hard, had an organization on the North Side, had sufficient money to run a good campaign. By the end of it, I thought I could get 28 percent of the North Side vote. I got 42 percent of the North Side vote. So you add 42 percent on top of 95 percent margins in the West Side and 90 percent edges in the East Side and the net effect was that I won with 62 percent of the vote. So I took office in 1981 with a lot of enthusiasm and a lot of hope.

The city was not as divided as I might have imagined, because the election victory was so solid, with 62 percent, which means that all of my opponents together had to share 38 percent. There were nine candidates, John Steen principal among them, but there was another major candidate that people forget, Jose San Martin's son, Jose San Martin Jr. In any event, the city was not as divided as I might have thought.

There were some very difficult issues hanging around. For example, COPS was calling for withdrawal from the South Texas Nuclear Project, as Austin had done. I had only said during the campaign that I would review it; I didn't say that I would do it and I didn't say that I wouldn't. So I had that to decide and bring to ground, and, then, any number of other issues. But what I found was that if I worked hard at bringing people together and followed that model of tripartite leadership for everything—a traditional San Antonio business-oriented person, an African-American and a Hispanic—we would create a sense of inclusion and also draw people out and get a lot of good ideas.

Frankly, as I look back on my mayoral years, I see them as divided distinctly into two parts: the first four years and the second four years, although I only ran for two-year terms. But it took me the first four years to sort of find my sea legs and to get fully confident in San Antonio.

The Orange Book

The key decision that I made, absolutely key decision, was literally through two pieces. During 1983, as I was preparing to run for reelection, I sat down at home and drafted a workbook. I literally did this at home, nights and weekends, and wrote out a workbook, a plan, for attracting jobs to San Antonio. It ended up being called the Orange Book by folks, because it described literally how we would proceed to try to bring jobs in five areas: the biosciences, computers and aerospace, agriculturally related, value-added tourism, and a fifth category—I forget what it was right this second—but a focus on five areas of creating jobs.

That was so well received by all the economic players in the community that I decided to take the area of jobs and create a similar work plan that dealt with other areas. And it became a kind of a goals for San Antonio document that covered jobs, yes, but also how we built up an educational base, and, in the end, about 12 areas of emphasis. In my second term, after having been elected with like 92 percent of the vote, that became Target '90.

Target '90 drew people together, 500 people, again tripartite leadership. Bob Marbut; Lou Nell Sutton, African American state representative; and Roy Kaiser, Latino cochair. The net effect was that we drew over 500 people together in these 12 committees, and they worked hard to set these goals for the future of the city.

Then we put forward a bond issue to begin to implement the first piece of this in the election of 1985. I had opposition by this point. Phil Pyndus decided to run against me, and people said don't run for reelection with a bond issue. It'll kill you. You'll be carrying the bond issue. They'll attack the bond issue. People will be mad about the bond issue. They rarely pass real strongly, and you'll pay the price.

As it worked out, it was the best thing I could have done, because it gave me something to fight for. I was able to go to the public and say, "Vote for me but vote for progress." I mean it was a burden to carry it, but in the final analysis, both I got elected, and I think my reelection number was in the 77 percent range, and the bonds passed. That experience gave me the confidence that I needed to do what needed to be done, to know that our coalition was intact, that it could hang together, that it could go into the teeth of strong opposition, that we could pass what we needed to pass.

So every year after that for the next four years we had some kind of bond or other progressive matter on the agenda. We passed about a half a billion dollars worth of bonds in the subsequent years. We passed the bond, the dome election, and we had a showdown, tough election, on a spending cap in the summer of 1986, which was, in some ways, C. A. Stubbs's high-water mark to that point. He had a plausible concept in a cap that would have limited city spending to an index of inflation in spending growth. The mistake he made was that he would have covered both operational as well as capital spending. We were able to prove to the city that capital spending needs to come in larger increments than inflation on occasion, and that this would really hurt the city.

COPS had always been pro-economic development; they just didn't understand it. Early on they were demanding huge wages, $15 an hour, and a company which had already agreed to come to town from Milwaukee, a tooling company, pulled out. It was clear at that point that they didn't understand. I think we were able to prove to them over the years that I was as serious about bringing jobs to the West Side like the glasses manufacturer that went into the industrial park across from Kelly Field, or the Levi Strauss plants that went into the South Side, or the companies that went into the East Side. We were working very hard to balance things out to where people had a sense of participation. And, of course, every one of those bond issues was about half and half. North Side versus the neighborhoods.

The business people always wanted roads. They wanted traffic congestion reduced, the priority on the North Side. In the South Side it was drainage, school improvements, school approaches, streets, sidewalks. Not only did I have to make sure that the southern sector did about as well as the North Side, but that each district had some priority they were seeking in it.

The result was that bond issues, which people said couldn't pass in that climate—Texas was going through a recession in the late '80s—passed with 70 percent, 65 percent, 66 percent, 61 percent margins. They only needed a majority, and they were well over 60 percent.

There was only one issue I supported and lost—fluoridation. And that was a miscalculation. I thought it was so obvious and so important, so easy to pass that I didn't wage a full-fledged campaign. As a matter of fact, the decisive debate on fluoridation I didn't even participate in. I had a commitment outside the city and I kept it. My wife participated in the debate, just as an example of how I didn't really take it as seriously as I should.

Well, you ask me, "What was the greatest disappointment of my tenure?" I think it was the inability, in the final analysis, to have a water plan completed when I left. After the spending cap, and after the successful bond issue of '86, I decided I wanted to try the same technique which had helped us produce Target '90 and so forth, and that is to bring all the players together and work on water. We had many successes, and there was a real sense of surge. River Center Mall had opened in '87, HemisFair Park was enr oute to being done. We had a plan to build the dome. About several hundred million dollars worth of freeway expansion was under way, as well as the double-decking of the downtown freeway system, plus the freeway to the west. Sea World was announced. Fiesta Texas was in the works. Lots of good things happening, but water had not been addressed.

No Scheduling Conflicts at 5 a.m.

I heard a speech by a gentleman who would later become my colleague in the cabinet, Bruce Babbitt, who had a similar water problem in Arizona. He said that what he did there was to call a meeting for eight one morning. People who didn't want to be a part of the water solution said that their schedules wouldn't allow it. He said, "Fine. Let's meet at seven." They said, "No, can't do it. Have a conflict with breakfast." He said, "All right. First meeting will be at five in the morning." No one could tell him they had conflicts at five in the morning.

And they came, and he held them together, and they stayed with it for years until they produced an Arizona water plan, which is in existence until today. It was essentially a trading of water rights from farmers to urban interests.

We used the same technique. It wasn't all that well-covered, although reporters were always there. But it wasn't breakthrough news every week. What we did was, we had the interests from the east, San Marcos and New Braunfels, join us, and the interests from the west, Uvalde and points inward, Castroville, join us. And every Thursday morning at 8:30 we met, from 8:30 until noon, for a year-plus.

We began to make real progress. We devised a plan that would have created water rights for the farmers out in the west, who could have sold their rights to aquifer water. And thereby San Antonio could have gotten the water it needed, but would have had to pay for it, and pay for the water rights, because we set the maximum withdrawal from the aquifer at the level that would protect the springs to the east.

It was doable. It would have required San Antonio to supplement its water supply beyond the aquifer with other sources. The principal source was the proposed Applewhite Reservoir, though we would have added a recycling plant at Braunig and Calaveras and used gray water for watering and industrial purposes and golf courses within the city, as well as purchasing water, possibly from Canyon Lake, a long-discussed but never implemented plan.

We came very close, and I thought we had a plan that was viable. But, frankly, the burden of carrying the politics of the dome through '88 to an election in 1989, which we won; my decision to step down, which I announced in September of '88; the personal difficulties ensuing during that time; and the effort to pass the library bonds as I left office in the spring of '89—all of that proved to be more than would allow me to go to the Legislature and make an all-out effort on a water plan. We came very close.

And then, of course, the ultimate blow was when the subsequent City Council allowed a referendum on a project that was already decided, and already under way, and allowed Applewhite to be defeated. That was a major disappointment.

There are a lot of reasons why I would have liked to have stayed another term, despite my decision to leave. There would have been two things, really, I think I could have done. Three things I could have done if I had stayed another several terms. One of them was the water plan. I would have loved to have seen that, and I certainly would have allowed Applewhite to be completed.

The second would have been to fight hard to get an NFL team into the dome. One of the teams now in Jacksonville and Carolina we should have had, in my view. The commissioner of the NFL later told me that they really had a lot of confidence that my team would build a dome and bring a team, but I wasn't there anymore and they just didn't look at San Antonio the same way. I hope it doesn't sound too immodest, but that's a fact.

The third thing I would have done is push the city slightly more in the direction of really prioritizing social services, youth, and educational matters, and not necessarily with city expenditures.

In my euphoria over passage of the dome I said I may change my mind about running for reelection. But Lila Cockrell had already announced. The business community had earlier asked, "Before we commit to Lila, are you sure you are not going to run?" and I said, "Yes, I'm sure," so they didn't hanker to the idea that after the dome was won that I would change my mind and run.

Who knows what would have happened if I had? It would have been a big fight in the community, because a lot of my supporters were already with Lila, and she said she was in to stay. And the community was, at this point, following the personal difficulties that I had, and that would have been some kind of factor. But in any event, I didn't run.

I'm very happy about things which would otherwise not have occurred without the dome, like having the NCAA Final Four, the NBA All-Star game, the Alamo Bowl. But my great hope was for an NFL team, and, unfortunately, some things have taken the direction in the last five years that, I think, don't have San Antonio quite as positioned as we were, say, in 1990.

The Kelly Field closure puts something of an economic uncertainty into the perceptions of the San Antonio future by outsiders. The water issues have not been resolved. The economy is growing, but not with quite the clarity of purpose, either in computers and telecommunications, or what biosciences that we were marketing before. I think the bloom is off the rose a bit.

I think the thing I'm proudest of is the coalitions that brought people together, who learned about each other and function as one city. Perhaps my perspective on that is tainted by the fact that I was so close to it.

But I really felt that we were bringing people together, and I was proud of the substantive progress that can be reported: the dome; the nuclear project completed and opened on our watch; the new sewer-treatment facilities; new gates and expansion of the airport; the work that the highway department did, the new freeway to the west; Sea World; Fiesta Texas; the Research Park; downtown Fiesta Plaza, I mean downtown River Center Mall; the river extension into the mall; the dome; the new hotels like Mariott River Center that opened with River Center Mall; HemisFair renovation.

All those things happened in those years. But the thing that I think I'm proudest of is that we did those things, and we didn't have to roll over anybody in the process.

That is to say, it was a city that had a sense for its destiny and was willing to walk together to do it. There was a sense that people were willing to sign on to an agenda, and I think that was the by-product of Target '90.

Nelson Wolff: *The Bureaucracy Evolves*

Nelson Wolff, who operated his family's lumber and grocery businesses, served in the Texas House of Representatives and Senate from 1970 to 1974, was elected to City Council in 1987 and served as mayor from 1991 to 1995. He was elected Bexar County Judge in 2001.

I was born on the South Side of San Antonio, over on McKinley Street, at a cost of $10 for the doctor to come to the house to bring me into the world. Most of my life has been in San Antonio, with some interruption when my dad was transferred to another place and we lived in Houston for some time. I have served in the Texas House of Representatives and Texas Senate in the early 1970s. It was shortly after I got out of law school at St. Mary's University that I ran for the Legislature. I lost a couple of congressional races, spent 10 years in the private sector after that, and came back and served on the City Council starting in '87 and then as mayor.

The seeds for public service were started when I was in law school. I ran for president of the student law body and won. Never thought about politics 'til then.

When HemisFair came I was 28 years old. I had been out of law school two years and the lumber business was beginning to build up and grow. You could feel some of the changes that were occurring in San Antonio then. But prior to that, San Antonio—I don't care whether you were black, brown, white or gray—was a relatively closed society from the economic standpoint.

When we started our business in 1961 out of an abandoned filling station on Roosevelt, we were in business for probably seven years before we could even get a loan. You might could have got a loan on an automobile or a truck, but you had to pay down 25 percent of the truck price and maybe finance 75 percent for two or three years. You couldn't get a working capital loan. So it was very, very difficult for any sort of a small business coming in and starting up.

The Hispanic community really hadn't begun to make strides in the economic or political areas. The Good Government League did a lot of wonderful things, and HemisFair was the major one they did. It was still a pretty close-knit group of folks that made those decisions economically, politically, the old money and the old families. I attribute the breakup of that to Charles Becker, quite frankly—it was really a revolution when he came in to be mayor—and to HemisFair. San Antonio starts to come alive a little bit. The new business class that's brought in becomes more powerful in the north part of the city, and you begin to see a breakup in the business community between the old and the new.

When Charles Becker made his run against the GGL, he put an organization out of business that had been in business for over 20 years, controlling the political makeup of the City Council. I've always considered his election a real watershed on the political end of it, and economically too, because it brought into power a lot of these guys who felt the city really wasn't progressing like it ought to progress.

Then in 1977, when the single-member districts came into being, the City Council makeup was changed. It's always interesting to remember that Henry Cisneros had run on the GGL ticket, at large, and had been

County Judge Nelson Wolff, a former legislator and mayor.

elected. Most people don't associate Henry with the old power structure. They were reaching out to find young voices they necessarily didn't agree with as the only way for them to survive. Of course, they didn't last very long after that, and then when it went to single-member districts it had a very profound effect on the way that city government operates.

I like the way single-member districts work. Had the history of single-member districts dated back to the '60s, when the city began to grow, you might have seen a different growth pattern because it was, quite frankly, not until the '80s when Cisneros became mayor that we began to address some of the inner-city problems, from streets and drainage and all those sort of basic infrastructure things. And had resources been distributed in a little different manner you might have seen a greater viability in inner-city and greater growth toward the south.

But by the '80s, the growth trends had become so strong about where they were gonna go, thanks to decisions made to put the University of Texas way out almost to Boerne and the decisions about the Medical Center, all made by people who really were not inner-city or South Side folks.

What if those institutions had been spread up some? What if, let's say, the Medical Center had been located along Loop 410, south of town by Palo Alto? Or if that didn't happen, what if the University of Texas at San Antonio had been located south, rather than north? Had single-member districts in the Legislature and the council been there in the decade of the '60s, it could have affected the growth patterns.

The UTSA decision was a very close-knit decision involving John Peace. I was on the periphery, just a legislator and really not smart enough or experienced enough to really be in tune to the powers that be. But I remember a lot of the speculations back in the era that friends of John Connally had land out there, that, indeed, he had an interest. Whether he did or not, I don't know, because these things were happening before a lot of this public disclosure, open records, financial disclosure. I can tell you some interesting stories of how we used to do the budget. But definitely John Peace made the decision as a key member of the Board of Regents, tied in, somewhat, with the governor's friends anyway.

Why Am I Doing This?

Do I ever wonder, "Why am I doing this?"

I think people come at these things from different perspectives. I think the guys who come at it or women who come at it do from the perspective of wanting to concretely accomplish something that will be remembered. Now, this is a lot of big ego here that is a driving force for some people, and it's the driving force for me. If you think that you're gonna leave any sort of a mark on what happened here, that the only way you can leave the major mark is through political service and being able to really accomplish some things. It is that ego of thinking that you are smart enough and talented enough to do those sorts of things.

I've always considered the first mark I wanted to be remembered for is the work that we did with the youth. You know, we've done a lot of things there, from the Coalition to the after-school programs, police athletics. And we've ranked youth even above police. You know, who would have ever thought of that? I've spent an inordinate amount of time and I tie that to the education issue, you know, picking up Henry's work with Education Partnership and the Goals 2000.

The second thing is, I think we've done a lot of good things to bring the crime rate down to some eight-year low. And historic buildings. Doing the council chamber, doing the courtyard there, fixing up City Hall on the outside that had deteriorated since 1895. And the library going up, and the things that we're doing there that I think are going to make a big difference in the inner-city.

And the other issue that I did mention though, but that has really come to the forefront, is this whole deal that we've done with NAFTA and the North American Development Bank and doubling the Convention Center and building an international building.

But it's been a real intense four years, and that's what's good about term limits. I like term limits because in knowing pretty damn well what I wanted to do, what I wanted to accomplish and knowing that I only had a set period of time to do it. And, then, when you can use that analogy that there is a shot clock on the wall, and that you either do it now or you don't do it. Let me tell you, that makes a hell of a lot of difference, a lot of difference to me, a lot of difference to the people sitting on that council, because I use the argument over and over with them: If you want to be remembered they'd better do it now 'cause they're not gonna be around.

Having an almost perpetually green council and mayor rather at the mercy of the bureaucracy is a concern. I can't tell you how arrogant the bureaucracy can be sometimes, even the arrogance in what is a very good bureaucracy. But if they think for one minute that they can run the city instead of the mayor and the council, they will.

Just for instance, yesterday we had on the agenda, with two day's notice, an issue dealing with employee health plans and how they would make their claims and whatnot. The employees had not been talked to, and the unions hadn't been talked to. So we made it very clear to the staff that we weren't going to be caught short in making that kind of decision, so I appointed a three-member council committee to review it. That's just one example of a very, very good bureaucracy.

But if they think they can run the city, they'll run it without the council and the mayor.

William E. Thornton: *The Rise of Neighborhoods*

Dr. William E. Thornton, an oral surgeon, served as Bexar County Hospital District chairman for 10 years. He was elected to City Council in 1991 and served as mayor in 1993–95.

The mayor in this city has one vote. We have 10 council members, so mine plus theirs, as I was one of 11. I had, by charter, no ability to set an agenda, literally, or for council meetings to determine what items will be discussed and voted on. But just like each of the council members, I had to get the concurrence of at least five others to join with me, to do that.

As I reminded myself and sometimes my colleagues, whereas each of the council members is elected by one-tenth of the city, the mayor is elected by the entire city. And so, because of that, the office is given more importance. But in getting votes and making things happen, I had absolutely no power over any of the council members, to make things move along.

With two two-year term limits, we're getting an almost perpetually green city council. By the time they learn how things work, they're on the way out. So certainly the power is shifting over toward staff, simply because they're the ones who have the planning department that they can assign to do research for them. They are the ones who can assign each of the department heads to simply spend their financial and human resources addressing this problem. We on the council, and I as mayor, didn't have that ability. And with the shorter terms for elected officials, we don't have time to build up a reservoir of involvement in issues and a memory of what's gone on.

Dr. William Thornton.

I certainly had a different agenda as mayor than I did as a councilman. Councilmen are basically having to deal with the delivery of basic city services—streets, maintenance, police, fire, garbage. The mayor has the ability to step away from that and from each of the single-member districts, and try to see where we are as an entire community. The mayor, I think, is the only person in city government, other than possibly the city manager, who has that opportunity.

I ran for City Council in District 8, the wealthiest part of our community. It's a part of our city where there's high voter turnout. It's the part of our city, when I ran in 1991, that we'd not redistricted or drawn the lines again since 1980. I had literally 200,000 citizens. It was a very large district. And it was the most organized district, in terms of neighborhood organizations, both voluntary and neighborhood organizations where it was mandatory participation.

So when I began to run, one of the first changes was that I was not interested at all in who the precinct chairmen were throughout the district. I was far more interested in who the leaders in each of the neighborhood groups were, because that was where the vibrancy was. That's where people were meeting, where they were talking about issues on a weekly, biweekly basis. And so, we were starting to see the rise of neighborhoods as a political entity that, quite frankly, in my opinion, needed to be dealt with.

Communities Organized for Public Service is separate. They were very much alike in that if you asked the question "What do you want?" both of these areas would say, "We want better infrastructure, better streets, better education for our children, and safer neighborhoods." It's amazing how they say the same thing. But, yet, there was a gulf between District 8 and District 5, where there was absolutely no communication. And, in fact, the perception in District 8 of what COPS was doing was not something that those people wanted to follow. But the truth is, they all organized for exactly the same reasons.

In District 8 I saw the voting numbers, just the raw power of where the votes were to be in those neighborhood groups more so than what could be driven or influenced by, in the past, simply coming in with a large amount of money and through direct mail, phone banks or whatever money would buy in a campaign, just bulling your way into a victory. It was more important to me to have the neighborhoods with me, for their votes, than it was to have the business community with me for their money.

Now, the balance was to try to gain the confidence of both groups. Once I got into office, that proved to be true. I had been a part of the business establishment, because in 1989 I chaired the Greater Chamber. But several changes were starting to take place. Also, in '89 we had a campaign to build the Alamodome. The battle there was won by the business community, but it was a close battle. And just citizens, those folks who represent the homeowners, taxpayers, not the business or the establishment part of our community, became organized and became a political influence from that point on. I'm convinced of that.

The old establishment members are "spent volcanoes," as Henry Catto told me, and which I thought was great. You know they're still there, they're clearly enormous, and yet they don't spew forth with the power they've had in the past, and whenever they rumble, everyone stops and looks to see what they're saying. I think those days are gone. I think the mayors and the elected leaders of this community, single-member districts, will certainly be grassroots campaigns, but I think the mayors are going to have to be more closely tied to people.

It would now be far more difficult, in my opinion, to do what was done in 1968. Look what was done in '68: HemisFair, UTSA, River Walk, Hospital District, Medical School. Those were all decisions made by the then-"establishment" that would be far more difficult to do today.

The election in '91, when I went in as councilman, also had a very spirited campaign of whether we should continue building the Applewhite reservoir or not. At that point, you had the business community, the establishment, the elected officials, all of these people who normally would have won elections in the past, saying, "We want this to happen." Yet, through petitions and through simple hard work and a lot of creativity, the citizens-based groups who were, quite frankly, on the outside of the establishment, won the election in '91. And Applewhite was turned down as a lake.

We saw a similar election in August of '94, on a second attempt to have a water plan for San Antonio. And it was the same lineup—on one side you had for the water plan the business community, the newspaper, the establishment, most of the money, all of the things you would call the "power structure of the city." Against it you had the people without money but with a great deal of passion and a lot of creativity on how they sold their message, and they beat the establishment again. And they not only beat them again, they beat them by a greater margin.

The two water issues were clearly not debated on the engineering of whether you can build a lake or do a water plan on the water issue itself, but the two elections were driven by political concerns. For completeness sake, I want to add, just legal concerns. But the biggest problem we had was a political issue, and it was distrust. The old days of the banks, the law firms, the accounting firms, the chamber, and the largest corporations coming together and deciding what we're going to do and then muscling it along with money, are gone. The Alamodome was the last one.

Now, look what else has happened. When the Alamodome election was going on in the late '80s, look at the number of banks we had in this city and look at the transformation in banks and in banking. Look at the law firms we had in the early '80s and then look at the transformation that took place through the difficulties of the '80s. Look at the accounting firms, the CPA firms. They, too, went from the Big 8 down to where there are even fewer. There was a total fracturing of the power structure in the matrix of what held this community together terms of legal, money, business, and political power.

All of those things came together where, at the end of it or at the beginning of the '90s, it was like a war where there was no one standing. As you looked around the horizon to see who was standing to lead us, there was no one. It was a difficult time for a lot of people, because I don't think they understood, those who had been in power before; they simply weren't in power any more.

And that's why, when I ran for election in '91, my interest was not those of previous power-brokers. I'm out there at neighborhood meetings, sitting in lawn chairs, fighting red ants. That's where the power was. Who had the ability to bring those groups together? As we all know in politics, the one who wins the election is the one who gets the most votes. And then at the end of that election, I can say, "I got the most votes." I think it has been a tremendous change in how this city is run.

You're not going to get rich. If you do deals for your friends, you're going to go to jail. Those are all the wrong motives anyway. The only satisfaction you can gain from this job is doing good things for San Antonio. But that's enough, and it's in enough quantity to offset all those negatives.

To be elected mayor cost me around $800,000, for a position that pays $50 a week. I did depend on the business community for the money. The person I was running against was Kay Turner, who had won the 1994 water election, had won the 1991 Applewhite election. She and others had won the fight against fluoride. And because of that time period, she had a much higher name ID that I did.

What's interesting was, in January of '95, just four months before the election, I did a poll, a good solid poll, a high number of people surveyed, and found that my name identification, after being on the Hospital District 12 years, chairman of the Chamber in '89, and a councilman for three and a half years, was 41 percent. It was lower than Kay Turner's because she had been in the previous campaign.

So, we realized that for me to win, the first thing had to be for people to learn who I was. In a mayor's race in a city this size, you've got to have money to buy television, to direct-mail. On the North Side to get out the vote, you have to do phone banks. So, we had to raise money. People say I barely beat Kay Turner, but the key word in that sentence is, "I beat her." She didn't get beat in '94; she didn't get beat in '91. I'm the first; she didn't get beat on the fluoride; I'm the first one to ever beat her.

5. East Side, West Side

Two days before HemisFair opened, the assassination of Martin Luther King Jr. touched off racial violence in several cities throughout the nation. There was none, however, in San Antonio or on the city's historically black East Side. Integration in San Antonio had occurred peacefully, as, after the fair, did the political ascendance of activists on the heavily Hispanic West Side. These five leaders explain the process.

Claude W. Black Jr.: *Blacks Join the Political Mainstream*

Longtime pastor of Mount Zion Baptist Church, Rev. Claude W. Black Jr. served on city council from 1973 to 1975.

I grew up in this community at a time when there was tremendous separation in terms of jobs, in terms of access to public facilities. You had to go to the Majestic Theater off of College Street, which was in the back door, and sit in the upper balcony. Same thing was true of the Empire Theater, and you could not attend the Texas Theater at all.

There was no restaurant downtown you could enter through the front door. If they made available to you any kind of eating facility, it was usually for the people employed downtown, and usually that was some backroom that was used by those persons who came in and needed food.

There were the health facilities, the toilets and all of this, usually substandard and marked "For Colored" or "For White." Fountains were marked "For Colored" or "For White," so you could not drink out of the same fountain. In addition to that, you had policemen, which was one the advances made in San Antonio—San Antonio had black policemen before many cities of Texas had black policemen. So that was the general picture.

Of course, schools were segregated, all public accommodations were segregated. The jobs that black people had at that time were largely jobs doing porter work in the downtown stores, serving as waiters and busboys in the major hotels, working for the railroad—many of them worked in the shops of the railroad and working for institutions like Alamo Iron Works. But you saw no black persons as bank tellers, in sales at the major stores.

Now, all of this is an indication of change. When you see a black person as a bank teller, you know that there's been change. When you see a salesperson at Dillard's or at any of the major stores, you know that that's a change. When you recognize attorneys—black attorneys—within the corporate structures, you know that's a change.

When I grew up there were no black firemen. While there were black policemen, there were no black firemen. I might mention the fact that also black policemen were not permitted to arrest white people. They were really there to maintain order among black people. Now you had some black policemen who would take the bull by the horns and do it anyway. You could understand that, because if you're building a structure in which you have defined blacks in inferior positions, you certainly would not expect them to use their police power on white people.

I think the greatest contributor to the change was the Supreme Court decision that was made around schools in 1954. And I think that stimulated the efforts and activities of blacks throughout this nation and throughout this

Rev. Claude W. Black Jr.

city, particularly, because it became a rallying point. We had to deal with the issue of the court and the actions of the school boards. So that built an organization around which we could make our thrust. Then along with this came an option for remedy.

Up to the time of Martin Luther King and the protest movements centered around him, blacks had looked, primarily, to the courts for remedy. I spent most of my young life giving money to the NAACP—my nickels and dimes—to correct the issue of inequity in the pay of public school teachers; there was a time when they did not pay black teachers the same they paid white teachers.

Then there was the participation of blacks in the Democratic primary, or any primary, because blacks did not participate in the primary. We could vote in the general election, but we could not vote in the primary. So those things had been carried to the courts and many of them had been won in the courts.

The poll tax was another handicap when voting, and that also led to a lot of the control that took place in the black community. There were those people who had enough money that they could buy—this was illegal—poll tax for individuals and maintain a whole goodly number of poll taxes, with the idea that those persons would be "instructed voters," because they had paid for the poll tax. So it had many implications. It was not just simply that blacks could not afford, it's a fact that the persons who had money could buy them for blacks and then control the direction of their vote.

San Antonio Lunch Counters Integrate

One of the most significant efforts to integrate lunch counters here was put around Joske's Department Store. There was a restaurant on the second floor of Joske's, a very nice restaurant, the Camellia Room. We set out to open that up. We stood in the door of Joske's and put a picket line around Joske's.

I can remember sessions that we held with the manager of that place who was caught between the protest movement that was having a negative effect on his business and the general sentiment of this community. He was having a hard time making a decision. While there were other people making decisions, he had a tough time. We set out to have people send in their credit cards and cancel their credit and walk around the store. Well, whenever you have a picket line around any public business, it has a tendency to affect the business in that place.

The outcome was the manager opened it. The contribution that the McAllister administration made to this whole task was that it set up a committee for voluntary integration of public accommodations, with restaurants particularly in mind. They worked in association with the council of judges.

The whole issue of segregation in the restaurants became an economic issue because San Antonio was then appealing to a number of foreign countries; Lackland Air Force Base was a training station, Kelly was a training station, and you had people who were not American blacks but who were just as black as American blacks. If they walked into a place and were denied, they had some remedy. This city became nervous about whether we can afford to have the government come down on us because the people who've come in here as part of the military were denied services.

While most of us knew that Mayor McAllister was a man who believed in segregation, we also knew that he was a man who had enough judgment to know that he wasn't going to let that stand in the way of the economics of this community. And so he supported this voluntary integration.

At that time those of us who were in the leadership of the movement of protest objected to that, because we saw it as a concession that would ultimately affect a legal position of integration. We did not want anything to get in the way. We did not want to go to the restaurants with the permission of the authorities, because those who gave you permission could also take it away. So, we opposed that, which was not always understood either by the white community, nor did the black community always understand this. We wanted it as a right, rather than as a privilege. And so we opposed that. And that was one of the dramatic moments in the life of change.

Fighting HemisFair

There was a group of us who fought the HemisFair. We fought it primarily because we saw in it an allocation of funds spent in a way that left no concern for what was going on in the East Side community. See, during that period the only positive thing that I can even remember is that they built a gymnasium on Lincoln Park. The expenditures, the allocation of resources to the East Side were terribly limited. There were a whole lot of needs never addressed during that period. The fair was regarded, and is still regarded, by the majority community as well-managed, well-handled.

But the excellence of the management did not have anything to do with the quality of life that the East Side experience. Even though it abutted on the East Side, there was no spillover, jobs or money. And for that reason we opposed HemisFair. On top of that, they built HemisFair with no back door to the East Side. You had to go all the way around to Alamo Street to get into HemisFair. It was a message to us that this is not for the East Side. And I think it was also a response of fear, because at that time there was a great unrest in black communities all over the nation. Los Angeles was having its fires; Detroit was having its fires.

I began running for the city council in 1963. I ran as an independent against Mr. Bremer, I believe it was, the handpicked Good Government

League candidate. I ran on the basis the right of representation of the black community. I think in some ways, the leadership of the Good Government League was impressed with the kind of race I had, because it was a better than average race.

I lost, but then I announced another time. This time they made a decision that they were going to have a black on their ticket. And that's the time they selected the Rev. S. H. James. Now, Reverend James and I were not running against each other, but everybody in the community knew that if he was on the Good Government League ticket they were going to satisfy their interest in black representation by selecting the person that had been identified through the Good Government League. So I lost the second time.

That was when the whole council was elected at-large throughout the city. And not only could blacks not win unless they were on the Good Government League ticket, whites could not win. Or Hispanics, if they weren't on the Good Government ticket. I mean that was a period of a powerful business community control of politics. But they claimed they were benevolent. And they claimed to be efficient. They ran on the issue of efficiency, you know. They were constantly talking about how much money they were saving the taxpayers.

I did turn my attention to the War on Poverty. I became a member of the Economic Development Board that was operating to take care of the funds that came from Washington to deal with the issues of poverty. At that time one of the guidelines for the administration of the money in the various agencies that had been approved was that they had to have poor people on the boards. Well, now, that was a controversial issue, because, as one man told me in the debate I had with him, "We are not going to change the decision-making process of this community." Which says to me that they weren't going to have any poor people on those boards.

There was still an assumption in those days that poor people didn't know anything or didn't know what was good for them, that kind of attitude. As a result, I was having great debates with those persons who had their centers of authority and power on the West Side and wanted to control the poverty program on the East Side. As a result of that, we were caught up in tremendous struggles against people who ought to be allies.

That conflict is growing more. And it's serious. I'm afraid that it is going to lead to some divisiveness in this community. It's going to lead, in my opinion, to a highly conservative black community, because they're going to find an ally in the conservative community who wants to continue to control the money, with the rising number of Hispanics in the community. That kind of alliance I don't think is going to service our city best.

Changing Politics on the East Side

The East Side, as we once knew it, has changed demographically. Blacks are about one-third, Hispanics about one-third and whites about one-third. And yet our problems have not changed that much. It's going to get tough. And so that's the kind of tension that you have here in San Antonio. You're going to drive blacks into the arms of conservative whites in this community. And, the fact is, whites understand that story because they've been dealing with power longer. They understand that better than persons who've just newly arrived at a point of power. People who are newly arrived at power want it all. I don't care what group it is, black or brown.

1973 is the year that, I think, that the Good Government League found itself in some political trouble. It was beginning to disintegrate. And because of my relationship with the black community, they were persuaded to ask me to run on their ticket. Sam James had stopped running a session before that, because Bob Hilliard came after James. I think Bob Hilliard had a lot to do with influencing them to ask me. I don't think, though, that influence would have meant that much if they had not had some political problems. They felt like getting me and my pulling the black vote would balance off what they were losing otherwise.

So I went back to the black community, and because I did not want to confuse them I said, "Now listen, this is what is happening. This is what they've asked me to do. What do you think I ought to do?" And they accepted the fact that I should run on the basis that my involvement in the War on Poverty had prepared me to deal with what was coming forward— revenue sharing, all those programs that were coming. I'd be in a better position to advise and counsel the black community if I were elected. So they said go on with it.

And so I went out and I was elected. Now, the interesting thing about it was that I was elected. There were five Good Government League people elected and four independents. At that time the council elected the mayor. The Good Government League took me for granted.

I was saying, "Well, what are they going to do with me?" But I wouldn't make any kind of statement. I was contacted by persons who were interested in being mayor. And I said, "I'll tell you what, I've got a formula. If you will make mayor pro tem a circulating thing moving from one councilman to another, and I become the first mayor pro tem, you've got my vote." The problem that the person had was that he made a commitment, I believe, I don't know that, but the person that I was talking to was Jose San Martin.

San Martin had the ambition of being this new era's first Hispanic mayor of San Antonio. But he had to make a commitment to Lila Cockrell that she would be permanent mayor pro tem, because she was setting herself up to become mayor. So he just totally ignored what I said. He didn't even respond to me on that. Then word got to Charlie Becker and the independents and they were ready to take my proposition. They were willing to accept that. So I said, "OK, if you're willing to accept that, then we're in business." So I voted for Becker for mayor of the city, and it made the difference, a 5-4 vote.

As a result of that, the next time around the Good Government League was debating whether or not they were going to put me on the ticket. I had a conference with a very strong person in the Good Government League, and they brought this person to talk with me to persuade them that I was an acceptable person.

But as I talked with that person, I just could see they were through with me. So I called Jim McCrory at the *Express-News* and said, "Jim, I got a statement I want to make. And that statement is: I'm not going to sit around here waiting for the Good Government League to decide whether or not they're going to put me on their ticket. I have a right as a citizen to run for that office and I'm running as an independent."

McCrory carried that on the front page. And it caught the imagination of these people. For some reason, there had been a deterioration, or a rejection, of the power that was being used by Good Government League. That was the real beginning of the end of the GGL. I got the largest vote I'd ever gotten, in that election, as an independent.

There is something about being a politician that can deteriorate the character of a man if he's not careful, because he's always looking for the compromise position, particularly if he's a minister. If there's one thing a minister has to do, he has to proclaim the absolute. People may compromise, but he's got to be clear enough in his own mind that he can proclaim the absolute.

I discovered I needed to get away from that. I had not selected a political office as my life's work; I had been drawn into it by the circumstances and conditions that I had to follow-up by getting into politics. And so, even though I have moved on, people still call on me in the black community, in terms of political life. And I've been out of it all these many years.

Ethel Minor: *The East Side Comes Alive*

Civic activist Ethel Minor served eight years as president of the San Antonio chapter of the National Association for the Advancement of Colored People.

I was born in San Antonio, reared in Columbus, Texas, and came back to San Antonio in 1944 and went to work for the federal government for 35 years, and retired in 1980. I was Equal Employment Opportunity specialist and managed two programs, the black employment program and the handicapped program.

I've been president of the local National Association for the Advancement of Colored People for the past eight years. I worked with them since the '50s. I drew up memberships, basically, or participated in some of the youth activities. We had the NAACP Youth Choir, we had a pageant on the river, we'd go out of town to some of the conventions, and things like that.

As I look at it today, in some instances I see us going back to the '50s, based on some of the complaints and things that we're getting in. You know, like the eating places here where blacks were being harassed, some of the things that are said to persons on the job, the way some of them are being terminated. It's just a number of things.

We have made great strides from the '50s until now. But there's just so much where people were kind of a lot of bigots, and they really didn't care because they felt like nothing was going to be done. I guess with the passage of the Civil Rights Act, it was kind of like you're holding this over my head, and they felt that people wanted quotas and we weren't looking for quotas, we were looking for equal employment or whatever. Just equality across the board is what people were looking for. And spending their dollars, they wanted to be treated like other citizens.

I can't say racism in San Antonio just completely went away. I don't think we'll ever see it completely disappear; that won't be in my lifetime, won't be in your lifetime, maybe in my grandchildren's lifetime. We're preaching peace and love and let's come together, let's work together. There's a certain portion of our communities—and I'm not just saying San Antonio, but communities around the country—still talking hate. Separatism.

Hispanics and blacks on the East Side get along about as well as they do in any other portion of the city. I have not seen or heard of any radical changes with them. If I would see anything, I would see more crack houses or dope houses, which are both the blacks and Hispanics too.

How is employment going for blacks? Slow. Very slow. We are getting a number of announcements for job vacancies. We just don't have a lot in our job bank as yet who meet a lot of the qualifications. I guess one reason is blacks weren't into a lot of the technological kinds of things and didn't get the number of years experience required. There was no future here, you know. They didn't even think about that kind of work.

How did HemisFair '68 affect East San Antonio? It was a happening, let's say that. A revival. There was a spirit, I guess, that you just

Activist Ethel Minor.

don't see too often. I guess it was the excitement, because nothing that big had been here in such a long time. It was just something unreal. I can remember so well, because my daughter even worked during that time. And it was so exciting. I guess I was down there every night. But as far as economic impact, everything kind of stays over on that side of the expressway. The only thing that they thought they were doing was St. Paul Square. And that has not really benefited black folks, as far as I'm concerned.

The main problem now is crime and what's happening to the family. The family structure is just not there. It's not close-knit like it used to be, where you could help rear your neighbors' kids or chastise them. Now if you dare say anything they might turn around and shoot you or might turn around and curse you out, where, in our times, you couldn't do that. That's one thing like they say about African tribes—the village is the family.

But I think the East Side is finally coming alive, you know? We just got the new Luby's over here, and it's been so crowded I haven't even had the opportunity to go over there and eat yet.

What they need to get off of the East Side is these darn pawn shops. They're nothing but fronts for these thieves. I know persons who have lost stuff to these shops, who have been in, identified their stuff and they can't get it. They've been reported to the police and all this. I think they need to clear all that out of here. They're trafficking in stolen goods, that's what it is, and that's aiding and abetting.

The black churches are becoming very integrated into our community. That makes a difference. I think more young people are turning toward Christianity, or turning toward the church. There's nowhere else to go, you know, so we come back to the Lord.

Joe Scott: *The Boss System Breaks Down*

Joe Scott is a political leader on San Antonio's East Side.

I've lived in San Antonio since I was 14, and I'm presently 65. I'm a Korean War military officer, retired, disabled, am retired from USAA and have been involved in economic development in East San Antonio. Now I'm president of World Technical Services, an organization concerned with hiring and employment of the handicapped.

It was racial segregation when I came here. San Antonio was not as bad as other cities, like my father lived in Fort Worth, where segregation was staunch. When I visited my dad it was a harsh city, in that in Fort Worth if a white person stands in the aisle, the black people pay their dime to ride the bus and get off in the front and go to the back door and go in. San Antonio never was like that. We sat at the back, but sat from the back forward, and that's the way it was.

Back of the Bus

Being a young rascal, I was put in jail in San Antonio before Rosa Parks on the bus in Alabama. What happened, there were these two black ladies seated at the back door, and I was on the way to school; I was a junior at St. Peter Claver's Academy. A friend of mine named Elsworth Summer and two white ladies got on the bus and—plenty of seats up front— and they stood in front of two black women, wanting them to move back. My friend said, "Look what they want those women to do." So I said to them, I said, "Plenty of seats up front. You don't have to move."

They, in turn, did move and sat over to the back seat. A neighbor of mine named Heiss was a white detective. He said, "You boys are inciting a riot here. I want you all move to the back and let them ladies sit down." My friend said, "Naw, you don't have to move back. You're sitting in the wrong seat anyway, 'cause you're sitting back of the colored side." I said, "Yes, you sure are, you need to move up front."

Political leader Joe Scott.

Then nothing was said. When we got to Alamo and Victoria Street, I think it's Durango now, the white women, who had been standing, moved up front and sat right behind the bus driver. So Detective Heiss stopped the bus driver and went off and used one of the call boxes to telephone for a paddy wagon, took every black person on the bus to jail in the paddy wagon. I was 16 at that particular time, in 1944.

My friend Elsworth was a senior, he'd just turned 18. When they took us down, they fingerprinted him, took him upstairs, they took me upstairs, they fingerprinted me and they let everybody else go. They said to me, "I want you to be in court to testify that this one"—talking about my friend—"was inciting a riot." They didn't do anything to me because I was a minor.

N. W. Graves lived at 1218 Florida, I lived at 1217 Florida. When the sergeant brought us up to put us in jail, N. W. Graves said, "Junior," he said, "What are you doing up here?" I said, "They wanted me to say that Elsworth was inciting a riot. I told them I wouldn't testify to that, and they told me they were going to lock me up, too." And Mr. Graves said to the jailer, "You'd better not lock this boy up, 'cause his momma'll come down here and turn this jail out."

So they just let me sit there, and I called Momma. She was working at the post office at night and then during the day she worked for a judge. So the judge and Momma came to get me out of the jail. I forget his name right now. Momma asked them, "What's my boy doing here?"

By that time she had called the sisters at St. Peter Claver Academy, and they all had come down to find out why I wasn't in school because they were very, very strict during that time. And Sister caught me by the ear and said, "Boy, what are you doing here?" And I said, "I'm not doing anything. I just wasn't going to testify to a lie without having an opportunity to tell how it really was."

So they were getting ready to get me out of jail, and I said, "Momma, I'm not going anywhere. Can't the judge get Elsworth out of jail too?" So he got us both out of jail. I went on over to St. Peter Claver, and when I got over there the sisters stood me up in front of the class and got the ruler on me, paddled me. But that's because of the fact that I was late and called my mother instead of calling them, 'cause they wanted to know. They really loved their kids, you know.

The charges against Elsworth were dismissed and we never heard any more from the incident. But the *San Antonio Register* came out, "Youth Jailed for Inciting Riot." Valmo's paper.

Valmo Bellinger, Rev. Claude Black, G. J. Sutton, R. G. Johnson, they were the powers-that-be. Anything they said went. They could say to the black community, "These are the candidates that we're going to vote for," and they voted for them. When John Connally was running for governor, well, he solicited their help. Don Yarborough was running against him. John Connally had just came out of the Kennedy administration and they decided they were not going to support him. And that is where the political process in East San Antonio changed.

That's when the change was, from boss politics to candidate politics. It was boss politics prior to the early '60s. In other words what they would say, no one would contest it. They would send that little letter out and say, "This is our candidate," and everybody would take that and go vote. And they would vote heavy. Like when Henry Gonzalez ran, well, he would get 98 percent of the vote in East and West San Antonio. That was the margin of victory against Labor.

You had what we called the Democratic Coalition—the blacks, labor, liberal whites, Jimmy Knight's group and that sort of thing. I was teaching in the Edgewood district then. Eddie Montez told the governor, said, I have a young man who will run your East Side organization for you. He's a teacher in Edgewood. So Eddie Montez came to me and asked who I was going to vote for. I told him I was going to vote for John Connally, 'cause he was a Kennedy man and I liked what Kennedy was doing. And he said, "Good. I want to take you down and introduce you to John Peace. We're

going to want you to head the East Side organization for John Connally."
So I said, "Well, where's Valmo and G. J., Reverend Black and R. G.
Johnson?"

He said, "Well, they're on the other side. Does that make any difference?" I said, "No, I don't know what I could do against that power." So
after I made that particular statement, well, I came down and they introduced me to John Peace and I met Governor Connally. And John Peace was
probably the best political mind, or one of the best political minds, that this
city has ever known. That was the change that destroyed the Democratic
Coalition and boss politics in San Antonio. That's where your political
change came.

Don Yarborough was quite a bit more liberal than John Connally. And
he had the Yarborough name. People had been voting for Ralph Yarborough
all the time, and they associated that name with Ralph Yarborough even
though they weren't related. John Peace said to me, he said, "Joe," he said,
"Your work's cut out for you." I said, "Yes, I guess so. Well, I just don't
know what to do."

Black Pastors Retain Influence

He said, "Who's your pastor?" I said, "Rev. Dr. P. S. Wilson." He said,
"Oh, that's the most powerful man in East San Antonio." Reverend Wilson, he's pastor of the largest church in East San Antonio—5,000 members. He said, "Talk to your pastor and see where he stands." So I talked to
him and Reverend Wilson said, "Joe, I'll be with you." So then I went to
the Baptist Minister's Union and I talked to them and they in turn said that
they would support John Connally, mainly because of the fact he was a
Kennedy man and in the Kennedy administration.

So we set up an organization. Then I talked to Ruth Bellinger, Valmo's
sister, and she said, "Joe, I'll help you." So Ruth and I and a lady named
Eva Hawkins and the ministers in East San Antonio combined together and
set up an organization that took, in that primary, on the East and in the West
side, 65 percent of the vote and 26,000 votes out of Bexar County, and
Connally won by 26,000.

When this boss system broke down and we replaced it with more independence, the churches, the pastors, still had a lot of influence. See, even
today, the black pastor comes from slavery. Their strength comes from slavery. During slavery the only person that could talk was the black preacher.

He's the only person that no one would take up a stick against, the black preacher. So down through the years he had this influence because his membership is really the voting strength of the black vote.

Those days are not over. They don't pack the wallop, but they do carry 50 percent of the black vote. The black vote is responsible for Nelson Wolff being mayor of the City of San Antonio. In 1991 I organized the ministers—Nelson and I went way back—and I worked awful hard on his campaign. I put together the black organization that delivered the black vote for Nelson Wolff. The issues have to be right because from the '60s on, the day that boss politics herds the black vote into a little cubbyhole and says, "This is the way it is," ain't there no more. You've got to have a candidate and that black vote has to be campaigned for and worked for. Nobody controls it. So I never wanted to be a boss politician. I've always been for what is right and what is good for the people of East San Antonio.

Since the system is changing, I can see the day when a white candidate could win what has been the traditionally black seat on City Council and in the Texas Legislature. A white candidate has to be a Democrat first, and now in the district in East San Antonio the white vote is conservative Republican. The Anglos who live in that district are fair people, and they said that we have representation everywhere and that the proper candidate, black candidate, who runs for office must be acceptable to them.

What would happen in a race if you have two candidates not acceptable to the whites, the whites will stay home and won't vote for either. Then it has to be settled between the blacks and the Hispanics. The Hispanic vote turnout is very low. The Hispanics have the numbers but don't have the households and the votes. They are ten years away before their families reach a voting age. They've got numbers now, but they don't have the voters. The day will come when they will have the voting majority in that district. But first of all is that the Hispanics must have a viable candidate. They're not going to vote for just any Hispanic because of the fact that he's Hispanic. He's got to have some credentials and he's got to be acceptable to them.

In East San Antonio, there's no difference between the Hispanic and the black. Of course, the majority of Hispanics in East San Antonio and blacks who live in East San Antonio have roots there and the roots are the same. They go to school together and some go to the same churches. The issues are there. Any candidate who runs on the issues and recognizes that the Hispanic is a part of the community will get the Hispanic vote.

HemisFair brought no economic changes or social changes or anything to the East Side because you had no leadership among black people here for economic growth. Being truthful, they're really not ready for it now. They talk about it, but they're not ready for it. The only way the blacks can be a viable economic force is you've got to have some black businesses. Integration diluted what businesses that we had.

You must remember that the social background of the black person is not business, it's 8-to-5. We are a servant class of people; we're not business. Since slavery we've been working as servants from 8 to 5, and we have very few, in San Antonio, who venture out into a business. When they venture out into a business, they venture out into a business that services blacks. We don't have an economic business base in dollars. Those influential business people we do have do not have a base in East San Antonio.

Ernesto Cortes Jr.: *The Rise of COPS*

Ernesto Cortes Jr. transformed San Antonio's politics when he organized Communities Organized for Public Service in 1974.

I was born at Santa Rosa Hospital here in 1943, graduated from Central Catholic High School, went to Texas A & M and to graduate school at the University of Texas. I got involved in the civil rights movement, and went to work in 1966 for the United Farm Workers, in the Rio Grande Valley, for a strike in Starr County.

After that strike was over, I worked for a year running the boycott for the farm workers. After that I was thinking about going back to graduate school, but my father died. I did a stint with the U.S. Commission on Civil Rights out of the Memphis Field Office. After that I went to work for a church in East Texas called Plymouth United Church of Christ, in Beaumont. I did voter registration and organized cooperatives and did some basic organizing.

From there I did a stint in Colorado with the United Church of Christ, then came back to San Antonio in 1969 to work for the Mexican-American Unity Council. I was in charge of economic development and housing for the Unity Council from 1969 to '72. Then I went to Chicago to meet with Ed Chambers, who was in charge of the Alinsky Training Institute. I went to work with the Industrial Areas Foundation in Chicago, Milwaukee, Lake County, Indiana, specifically East Chicago.

Organizing COPS in San Antonio

I came back to San Antonio in January 1974 to put together what became the Communities Organized for Public Service organization. In July 1976 I went then to Los Angeles to work with another organizing effort in East L. A. I was not living here, but would come in on a regular basis. After a year of that then I began to supervise development of what became known as the Metropolitan Congress and Alliance, with Sister Pearl Caesar.

Then I began also working with El Paso and Fort Worth, sponsored many efforts there. In 1981, I believe it was, I moved the organizer from COPS, who was Robert Rivera, to El Paso with the El Paso Inter-Religious Sponsoring Organization (EPISO) organizing effort. Christine Stevens moved to be the organizer here in San Antonio, and I worked with her and with Robert Rivera.

In 1982 I moved to the Rio Grande Valley and formed an organization called Valley Interfaith. I stayed in the Valley for three years and then moved to Austin. By that time there were organizations in the Rio Grande Valley and Houston and Fort Worth and El Paso.

Essentially the biggest change in San Antonio over the last 25 years is that San Antonio was run by a fairly well-knit oligarchy of well-off, very well-off people, all of whom, mostly whites and WASPS, lived in the northeast quadrant of the city and kind of dominated the politics and economics of the city. Some of them had a fairly developed sense of noblesse oblige and had some commitment to the city. But it was also to maintaining a very dominant position, a kind of oligarchy. Well, they were an oligarchy. Not a whole lot of time and energy and attention or resources got put on the older areas of the city.

They would argue that they developed this kind of city manager–councilman form of government, which came out of what they felt was a corrupt machine city commission system that existed prior to that. But the difficulty was, notwithstanding whatever you could argue about that commission system, whether it was inefficient or whatever, it did provide some modicum of services and accountability to the older areas. The reform system they brought in, the council-manager form of government, was driven by providing services to that northern part of the city.

So you began to see some significant changes, it seems to me, in the '60s, slowly, gradually. But, of course, for me, the biggest change is with the development of the COPS organization in 1974 and the fact that you began to see a built-in, sustainable, long-term process of involving people.

In the '60s preceding COPS, there was a whole fight over whether or not there was going to be War on Poverty. That kind of raised issues. There was a whole struggle to remove the poll tax. There was the work that people like Henry Gonzalez and Albert Peña and Joe Bernal did, in terms of trying to get people to think about things differently. And I think all that was very, very important. So there was a lot of awareness of the fact that there was a gap between what ought to be and what was. There was some impact with things like Model Cities and some of the poverty programs of the '60s.

COPS organizer Ernesto Cortes.

I wasn't here as much in the latter '60s, but the people I cared about were on the side of keeping the hospital downtown and felt the decision to put the Bexar County Hospital where it is now was a decision to locate away from the older areas and a decision to subsidize development on the North Side. But I think more pivotal decisions were to build San Antonio Ranchtown and what that meant, in terms of extending services to that area, and placing the campus of the University of Texas where it is. That really sent signals of withdrawal of commitment to the older areas, withdrawal of commitment to the inner city.

After those decisions, you began to see the Water Board deliberately pursuing policies of extending services to the older areas, the City Public Service Board following suit, etc., so that there was a real decision to try to engage in this whole sprawl dynamic in growth-management, and away from growth-management.

We in COPS cut our teeth on those fights. We went over the Water Board studies and analyses. We read letters Congressman Gonzalez had written about the whole question of the City Water Board becoming the sole purveyor and why that was important. We did an analysis of the impact of private water companies that were set up by people like Cliff Morton and John Shaeffer and all those guys, and the negative effect that was having on San Antonio's situation.

So those were defining moments for us. Ironically we got into it almost offhandedly, because we found out that the City Water Board was going to apply for money from the Community Development Block Grant program for water main replacement in the inner city. We were asking the question, "Well, why should they want money from CDBG for main replacement when, in fact, that should come out of the resources that the rate-payers were giving them?"

We found out, as we began to do further work, that the money the rate-payers were using for main replacement and main extension was primarily outside the city limits, so they were saying, "Well, we couldn't do the inner side of the city limits because we were doing two-thirds of those dollars were being spent outside the city limits." And that's when we began to see the huge inequities in that kind of a policy.

I always had a kind of intuitive feeling that something was not right about the city. From working for the farm workers and meeting with people like Gilbert Padilla, learning how they started off, finding out their roots with the Industrial Areas Foundation, the Alinsky Institute, reading that stuff, doing research on the economy.

When I was in graduate school I would do research on poverty and inequality in the United States, just kind of looking at all the studies that have been done on the existence of poverty, and what is poverty, and what are the strategies to deal with it, whether it's manpower or education or job training or income maintenance or early childhood intervention strategy— just looking at all the things that people argue need to be done in order to be able to deal with poverty. I came to the conclusion that what the Industrial Areas Foundation was talking about doing made a lot of sense to me. So the decision to organize COPS was a long time coming.

Well, the first step was to raise the money so I could do it, organizing for three years. It was just kind of stringing together small amounts of money. The next step was to begin to look for leaders. I did about 1,000 individual meetings, one-on-one meetings from January until August of 1974. I would go to the pastors first and ask for some names of people, go to school principals, go to unions, just everybody I could find, just kind of tell them I was working for the sponsoring committee to find out whether they would be interested in building a broad-based organization which would deal with a lot of these kinds of issues, whether it be utilities or streets.

There was a lot of skepticism, initially, on people's part. They were wondering, what is this really all about? Is this a political thing, or what is it? Then we were putting together what we call "small group house meetings," from there doing research actions and then beginning to put together larger, bigger public actions on issues like flooding, initially, getting garbage cleaned up and sidewalks fixed, and, out of that, putting together what we called the COPS Counter-Budget—$100 million worth of improvements to the inner-city areas—then getting on the Counter-Budget agenda, moving that and finding that we had issues like the City Water Board's request to deal with. Which then got us into larger questions.

The First Confrontation

The first action we ever did, I think, was with Melvin Sultenfuess, who was then director of Public Works, which involved an area where the kids were walking in some water and some dangerous and hazardous areas. The people were concerned about it, so we had meetings, built a sidewalk and a fence. Leaders mostly came out of the one-on-ones. I'd sit down with somebody and say to them, "Well, could you introduce me to somebody else?" Then they would refer me to other people.

We started out with a lot of small stuff and we went into the "COPS Counter-Budget," putting together streets, drainage and other kind of public improvements. We went on that one for about a year. Then we really got kind of noticed over our fight with the City Water Board, because then we went from being considered more than just a group concerned about its own agenda, its own interest, to one that is concerned about what happened to the city of San Antonio, and we began to get the Water Board to change its policies.

There was a lot of tension and polarization because we were pretty tough, and we wanted to be. When we didn't get some response from the political establishment we went to the corporate community, and we did some things which were kind of shocking—the tie-up actions at Frost Bank, the browsing action at Joske's of Texas, and that brought a lot of reaction. I mean, we were attacked for shouting down the city manager, Sam Granata, and there was a big editorial that said, "Don't shout." There was a recall petition over the mall over the aquifer. The people who were supporting the mall and wanted people to vote yes ran a commercial: "San Antonio City Controlled by Mob," and, "Don't Let COPS Dictate To You." It was always that kind of stuff early on.

As much as anything, I think the beginning of the turning point was winning on the single-member City Council districts, changing the structure of the city-government from at-large districts to single-member districts. COPS played a particular role in that. It's hard for me to say if there's any particular event, or it's that just after a while people began to recognize it would be better to negotiate with us. That's what we had always wanted. We weren't into confrontation for its own sake, we were into confrontation to get people to sit down and negotiate.

I think we changed public policy significantly in several areas. Number one was to increase the tempo and pace and direction of public spending, in terms of really making an investment into the neighborhoods. Number two was changing the whole structure of city government. Number three was getting the utility companies to really redirect and change their policies toward much more inside the older areas of the city, inside Loop 410.

The '80s were a bit of a disappointment, because there was a movement away from some of those, but the '70s were a pretty heady time for COPS in that sense, showing the chance for San Antonio to really be a different kind of city in a very fundamental kind of way, and to really make the kind of investments in people, in areas, in geography, and to become a much more open and participatory city. I think that continued, clearly through 1984. In 1989, I think it was still there, but the luster was off a little.

It changed for all kinds of reasons; they decided, because of the Reagan years, because the good mayor, Henry Cisneros, decided he wanted to be into this kind of pro-growth kind of stuff. I think he made some bad decisions supporting South Texas Nuclear Power Project, the domed stadium, some of the big water projects. And I think there was too much credence given to what I think is an outmoded theory of trickle-down growth, that we need to do these big-time projects and they'll produce the jobs, the people will come to us and we can lure companies to come to San Antonio by everything from tax incentives to what-have-you.

I think it's been remarkable, actually, where things have gone in relation to what we expected at the time. Most people thought that an organization of its kind could not last longer than seven years, certainly not with any vitality. Its capacity to regenerate and renew and meet new challenges has been remarkable, and has met if not exceeded my expectations.

But to me that's not the question. The real question is, "What do we do to meet the challenges of the 21st century?" And those are daunting. I think you're going to see more inequality in the United States, so you can say that the bottom half of the labor force's wages is going to continue to go down in real terms and the top 20 percent's wages are going to go up.

What can be done about it? Several things. You can do more Project Quests. You can do public sector employment, recognize that there are jobs for people who are low-skilled that need to be expanded. I'm suggesting absolutely that. I'm suggesting that right now what we need to be concerned about is maintaining a high level of aggregate demand; we're not doing that.

Then we need to increase the minimum wage.

Helen Ayala: *New Communication*

West Side political activist Helen Ayala served a term as president of Communities Organized for Public Service.

I was born on Barrera Street, right by where the Tower of the Americas is, in 1945. We moved into the Edgewood community when I was about two years old, and I always had a lot of family living around me. I lived on the street where both my grandmothers lived, and three aunts, so we occupied a whole block. We didn't have any fences. We lived like in a commune. We all washed together on Monday because we had to share the water. We didn't have any water, any infrastructure for water. So everybody ironed on Tuesday.

When I went to school, the school didn't have any indoor toilets. All through fourth grade we didn't have enough facilities, so I only attended school a half-day. When I went to junior high—it was a new facility—the best thing I remember was that I took the longest shower.

We had a lot of parents participating with the kids, we had a lot of family support. But I do remember we had no infrastructure. One time when my parents bought me a beautiful pair of shoes I wanted to take them to school and show them off. Well, I lost them in the mud when I had to cross this creek and there was no bridge. So, I went right through, and the mud got my shoes. When it rained real bad we couldn't cross, so we didn't go to school. Very rural kind of conditions. Things got better, in a way, but they never really changed. We still had the water problem for years.

We had a man who would come by with barrels full of water. We had to purchase the water. We kept some barrels that we used to catch the rainwater, so we had nice, healthy hair. That was true until, say, 1958, when we started getting water. We also had to operate with propane, butane. We didn't have gas coming through. When I came in my first year as city councilperson, I found this street in my community where people didn't have water and didn't have gas. That was within my council district, about two blocks away from Kelly Air Force Base.

When I was president of COPS—I was the sixth president—most of our issues were dealing with drainage and infrastructure. Drainage was really one of the first big issues for COPS. In fact, I lived a half-a-block away from where the first big drainage project was done with COPS. I grew up around that area. We're still working at that, but things have changed. I don't think children have those conditions to go to school under. One of my priorities is to make sure we have streets and sidewalks that will take care of the children's needs.

I got married the day after John Kennedy got killed. My husband is a San Antonio police officer, so he had the opportunity to see him when he visited San Antonio, and then the next day when he was killed it was certainly a very sad day. It was too late for us to change anything about our plans, so we went ahead and got married.

I was in my community for quite a few years. I never really did anything except raise my two children, and, being married to a police officer, that's what I was doing, being a good wife and active with my children. I was always active in the church. In fact, I used to be religious class educator at St. Jude's, which at the time was called St. Augusta Catholic Church. I was the first woman president of the Catholic Youth Organization at St. John Berchman Church.

I was out in the yard one time, and there was a little girl who came crying and told me she had a real bad experience with a man coming out of a bar. Well, I was outraged, so I tried to find out what was going on. I found out that there were nine bars in a two-block area. The children couldn't go to school without having to go through that. So I proceeded to find out or

San Antonio's outgoing COPS President Helen Ayala bids farewell in 1988.

how we could shut them down. That's when I started getting active in COPS, 'cause in my church we didn't have a COPS organization. It was the one parish in the West Side that had not been a part of COPS.

Moving the county hospital to the North Side had an impact on me through my grandmother. She was diabetic and would come to the clinic over at Robert B. Green Hospital and get her appointments done. I used to come with her. As I got older my grandma really didn't go to get checked anymore because the new hospital it was too far.

Out in the Edgewood community there wasn't that much impact from HemisFair, except that when the site was cleared we had an influx of people moving into Edgewood. Establishment of UTSA on the North Side never touched us. Forming single-member City Council districts didn't impact me, personally, but overall I could feel the excitement that there was something going on we were a part of, as opposed to other council elections.

Looking back, I see the difference it makes for someone to call me and say, "I need my garbage picked up, I got missed," or, "I need help with a dog." They have a place to make good contact. Before, there was no way.

I got involved with COPS in trying to close the bars on that street, or at least to regulate something about the presence of children around the area and how they had to operate. People shouldn't have to live like that. We tried, unsuccessfully, but I learned a lot. I learned that I had to work with other people to get the same goal. I think the knowledge I gained from COPS taught me and a whole lot of other people how you empower people to have voice in your government.

Then I started working on other issues. One was the economic development issue, another the education issue. See, up to that point, many others, like myself, didn't know how education worked, and how your tax base in your district affects your funding and the level of education you'll have when you have dollars coming in to support your school system.

In Edgewood we have minimal businesses and a lot of public areas that are not generating any taxes for your area. Now that we have the computer age and children having to become familiar with computers, and if they're not available at your school you're lost. You've fallen through the cracks. And there are other barriers that keep you from that. I was the COPS chairperson for economic developments for Edgewood, and learned a lot.

I think the whole issue was a conflict of two entities looking at the issue. At the time I used to have discussions with Mr. Quincy Lee about it. I learned a lot from him, and I'm sure he learned from me. It wasn't so much about maybe even differing. It was not understanding each other.

I think the whole COPS experience has been one of education for one-to-the-other, because if you don't talk you don't communicate. I think that all these years now there's been that communication. Not just myself as having been an ex-COPS leader, but perhaps even now, with the current COPS, it's a matter of exchanging those views. There was a time in San Antonio when you couldn't do that.

That's where the change in the city has happened—not because you are forced to do this, not because you have legislation that you had in single-member districts, not because you have policies that changed, but because there is communication now. I think that's where everybody wins. You don't have to agree, but you communicate with each other, and I think that's the difference.

6. Reflections

HemisFair's repercussions permeate modern-day San Antonio. Large numbers of people brought to San Antonio by the fair stayed, leaving a profound human legacy in fields from business to the arts. Here seven citizens reflect on various aspects of the fair's legacy.

Joe Cosniac: *A HemisFair Immigrant*

Restaurateur Joe Cosniac, born on the Austrian-Italian border, is one of many San Antonians first drawn to the city by HemisFair.

Restaurateur Joe Cosniac.

I first came to San Antonio after Expo in Canada 1967, and was here a few months prior to the opening of HemisFair in 1968. Before being in Canada I lived in France. I came for the Belgian waffles concession at HemisFair, and also moonlighted a bit as a waiter at the Bavarian Beer Garden to make expenses. I came with Nick Pacelli, who died in 1993. He was working at Original Joe Pizzas for Josef Freed, who used to own the University Club and who recruited him at Expo in 1967, and he worked at Expo and I worked at Expo.

After HemisFair '68 I went to Mexico City for the Olympics and then went back to Canada. Since I was accustomed to the weather in Texas, I decided to come back. I didn't want another winter in Montreal. I wasn't aware that when you live in a cold climate all your life, that's how you think it's going to be. When you change climates then you change your mind how things are.

Nick and I actually drove down here. We didn't know what we were going to do , maybe work. But it came about there was a place for rent for about $600 a month. It was just a box. Used to be a barbershop, and it was a meat store. That's where we opened our original Paesano's Italian restaurant. As we grew the city grew. When I opened I was barely 22. So the people coming here were still in high school and those people today got families, they've got grown kids and they've got some grandchildren. So we're dealing with three generations.

One of my customers is Orel Hershiser. I met him here because Jamie Byars is from San Antonio—he came to play for the San Antonio Missions, or San Antonio Dodgers at the time. We don't treat him as a baseball player or as a celebrity; he's just another customer. I think over the years what's made this place successful is the little bitty guy. We've always gone out of our way to make him feel very, very special.

And the so-called famous or infamous people, whatever they were, we just treat them like anybody else. Rupert Murdoch came in; he was just a guy with an English accent. I had no idea who he was or what he was. So today I've still got a good relationship with the guy, because it's not based on his accomplishments, it's just based on him coming through the door as a customer. So he may be sitting there, a very wealthy man, another guy may be just a laborer, but there's no difference. They're still tables apart. Eating the same type of food. It doesn't matter.

What makes a restaurant is energy and electricity created by customers. Like here, I know everybody who comes in, so I try to put them all basically in the same area, because there's some kind of show. People are insecure and want to be seen, and everybody likes to know so-and-so, and they want to see this one. So it's a social thing. You try to keep the old people basically in the same area so they can see each other. If you separate them, there's no atmosphere. You've seen it!

On the River Walk, the market is totally different. That's why I went there. I've got Rio Rio, Zuni Grill and Paesano's. But we still get local people, because they like the food, they like the atmosphere, but the menu's totally different. The only thing similar is the name, basically. There may be three or four dishes similar.

Since the late '60s and early '70s the town has changed, not so much the restaurant business. Before, you dealt with a city and a community based within Loop 410, where the city ended. You know, John

Charles' Steakhouse was out in the wilderness, out on the ranch. Now Loop 1604 is almost downtown. The new center of the city is 410. So you have a different clientele. In the old days, the people coming here in the late '60s, early '70s, as well as right up to the mid-'80s, were all local. You could come in here and know everybody.

But as the city expanded it brought new people into town. I mean, there's people north of Loop 1604, Huebner Road, I-10, they never heard of this restaurant. They don't care about downtown. They may go to downtown four or five times a year for a special event where they go there when the Spurs play or to the Majestic.

But San Antonio's still got the heart, from Loop 410 in. If you look at the rest of Texas, I mean, it's nice and everything, but there's no other town like San Antonio. From Loop 410 in, with the whole down-town—Market Square, the River Walk, the cathedrals—it's got some heart and soul, with the Mexican culture here. It's great.

James R. Dublin: *Old Families to New Money*

James Dublin, president of the public relations firm Dublin & Associates, has long been involved in the city's economic development.

I came to San Antonio in 1968 when I transferred in as a junior at Trinity University from the University of Texas at El Paso. My family and I visited Trinity, for the first time, on Easter weekend, which is when HemisFair opened, the very weekend it opened. They had just rolled the sod out the day before, and you could see the sod was just laying on top of the dirt. So that as it happened the very first day I ever saw where I was going to school was the day that HemisFair opened.

One of the jobs I've had since 1975 has been to help the Economic Development Foundation promote the city, to attract new business. As a result, I've been "selling" San Antonio for a long time. So I've thought about it a lot. One of the things that I think San Antonio was, back then, is more of a Southern city than a big Texas city. The Texas cities are Houston and Dallas, kind of brawny cities and free-enterprise entrepreneurship, "Come in here, anything you want to try you can go try."

San Antonio was a more Southern city. It had a totally different, slower flavor, famous in history, a much tighter society for the capitalists but also a much tighter business society, of the old families that still owned the business community. Newcomers weren't necessarily welcome.

One thing that's happened since then was in 1975 or '76, when the Legislature passed the bill that allowed a bank in one city to open a bank in another city. Everything had always been very local. So for the first time banks from other cities—specifically Houston and Dallas—came to San Antonio.

You had an infusion of people looking to finance people, most of them real estate developers. Real estate development hadn't happened nearly at the level it had in other cities in Texas. Real estate developers tend to be newer people, maybe a little rougher, much more risk-taking than old groups that had been here, some of them for a couple hundred years. Everything had been the same for decades and decades.

Jim Dublin, left, with Economic Development President Ralph Thomas in 1975.

So this new group of people, coupled with outside banking money, made a tremendous difference in the business community alone.

These real estate developers—Jim Dement's a good example—fought against the old establishment. They weren't welcomed into the clubs. They had not had a great deal of success in getting loans, risk-taking kind of loans, which is what a real estate development loan is, from the existing banks. So that friction grew and began to cause a bit of a schism in the business community between the old guard and these new people.

The outside money funding this new group of people fueled all this growth. When I got here, North Star Mall was at the extreme northern frontier and had only just been opened. When you said you were going to North Star Mall, you may as well have packed a picnic basket and gotten on a horse and tent and you were going to spend three days, getting there and coming back. It was just way beyond where it was usual for normal people to go. There used to be a restaurant out on San Pedro called Casey's John Charles Steakhouse. You'd go out past Hollywood Park and that was so far in the country, and he had such a bad sign that after dark you virtually couldn't find the place.

So one of the big things that happened was the new money, which came in to serve these new people who weren't getting served by the existing establishment. On the business community side of things, that spawned the creation of the North San Antonio Chamber of Commerce in 1974. That was a time when some of these new people, with Jim Dement as a leader, were making noises and pushing and wanting to be more engaged in the leadership of the Greater Chamber and they weren't getting in, or they'd decided they weren't getting in.

One day that year, maybe in late spring, they decided to form their own chamber of commerce as a direct response to the fact that they didn't think they were getting the attention they deserved from what they perceived to be, quote, The Downtown Chamber.

I worked for the Greater Chamber from 1973 to '75. My work history was, get out of Trinity in 1970 in December and become the first and the entire editorial staff for Lewis Fisher's new *North San Antonio Times*. I painted the walls, I moved in the furniture, and we had to make a decision on how many bylines we would give me each week because I wrote every story in the paper, this weekly suburban paper. He wrote the editorials and worried about the ads. Then I went to Our Lady of the Lake University in public relations and development, and in 1973 got a job in public relations at the chamber.

General Robert McDermott was the chairman of the chamber in 1974. He found himself in a situation where, because of the Oscar Wyatt–inspired energy crisis that we had the previous winter, the city, which had been funding the chamber's Industrial Advertising and Economic Development staff, cut that contract out. The reasoning was, why are we trying to attract new companies to this city when we may have brownouts for our existing citizens?

A Confrontation for the Economic Development Foundation

So nothing was being done on the economic development front. What McD did in the summer of '74 was create the idea of the Economic Development Foundation that would have everybody as a member, including the Greater Chamber and the North Chamber, both of which became members. He went around and raised the money to do that. What also caused the need for an EDF-type thing was that the end of the Vietnam War meant a downsizing at our bases, particularly Kelly.

Another major thing that happened, of course, was the rise of Hispanics to political power with the demise of the Good Government League and creation of single-member council districts. There began a quick battle with the developer group, which was probably totally predictable, South Side versus North Side.

The big confrontation came when COPS decided that the Economic Development Foundation, which had been formed about three years previous, was selling San Antonio, in their words, as "a cheap labor city." The COPS people had seen something, I think in *US News and World Report*, and they got confused between median wages and family income, a vastly different number. But they picked on the business of $15,000, saying that EDF should never bring in a business that paid any less than a minimum of $15,000 a year for any employee.

This was in 1977. I think I was making maybe $16,000 that year, working for a public relations firm out of New York at the time. So, $15,000 was a lot of money then.

A few days later COPS had an annual convention in the Arena. There were 10,000 people there. They hung in effigy three EDF leaders, Gen. McDermott, Bob West and Harold O'Kelley. These were guys who thought, three years previously, they were doing a good thing, in trying to attract new business, and raise this money, and uniting the business community, which had been divided on the north and downtown lines, and now they were referred to as "robber barons."

It was an absolute media circus. The national publicity in magazines like *Forbes*, and in the *Wall Street Journal*, was deadly. It stopped industrial prospects from even looking at San Antonio. Our competition was only too happy to Xerox these stories. I think the *Wall Street Journal*, in a page one story, had a headline something like "Second Battle of the Alamo." The *Forbes* headline was something along the line of "The City That Shot Itself In The Foot."

It finally resulted in Vietnam-type peace talks where there were discussions about a neutral site to have a meeting. The shape of the table? Could the meetings be recorded or not? How many representatives from each side would be allowed to meet?

It was decided that meetings would be at the YMCA downtown and that there could be tape recordings, and that each group, after these sessions, could make its own statement—which the other side would of course tape record, so no one could question what was or wasn't said. The media waited breathlessly outside the door of each meeting. I think there were three of them over a period of about a month.

In the final analysis, a truce was declared and they quite literally signed, on a stage, in a parking lot, to great fanfare, that there was peace in our time, before TV cameras and everything. I believe it was about March of '78 that it finally was officially resolved, with this literal peace treaty being signed. The net result led to the formation of United San Antonio in 1979 and 1980. But people had to learn to deal with each other. And they had to learn to accept the fact that we've got to look at the whole city all the time. And so you got bond issues, you got money being spent around the city to fix streets and drainage, which was the first concern that the COPS people had.

Too, you got neighborhood associations throughout the city in some ways are modeled on COPS, because people saw that common folk could make an impact, and many of the people in COPS were Kelly workers and just people who lived on the South and Southwest side. That did spawn things like the Metro Alliance and it spawned neighborhood associations now a political force all by themselves that also know, quite frankly, how to work these politicians and work the press.

But in all this time, there was virtually no industrial activity, because San Antonio was in effect blacklisted. When companies can decide where do they want to go there are a lot of economic factors, but stability, community stability, is a big factor. They are not going to go where the city's having a war about how to do economic development, and that was how we were perceived, even when the war was officially over. There began to be some more economic activity, but there was still this general malaise in terms of we just can't seem to get anywhere, for the most part, in attracting new business.

United San Antonio Gets Things Going Again

So we formed United San Antonio, with three sector chairs. The EDF devoted its advertising budget to a series of single full-page all-edition ads in the *Wall Street Journal*. Very expensive thing to do.

But we decided that in the very first working day of 1980, the new decade, which was January 2, we would have this ad on that Monday, or Tuesday, or whatever it was. We would say, "San Antonio Is Back! We're here. Here's what United San Antonio, here's what we are all about." Then we ran eight or nine different ads talking about the city for economic development and a community perspective.

At the same time, some of these computer companies that had been looking all turned all at once, and bang, bang, bang, we had two or three industrial announcements. And that got us going again. You go through 1980, you come up to 1981. Henry runs for mayor against John Steen, who was the chairman of the GGL, and that was the last gasp of the GGL.

I remember going to the Houston and Dallas bureaus of the national press, because that's how San Antonio is covered. I went to the *New York Times* and to the *Washington Post* and to *Newsweek*. I said, "You need to come over here in May, put it on your calendar, here's the election date in San Antonio in May of 1981, 'cause it's going to be a fundamentally different place." People had begun to hear about this young Henry guy, but what about him? And I said, "There's going to be a sea change in San Antonio in May." They all came over, and of course he won with 60-some percent of the vote, and away we went.

So the Cisneros emergence was a huge part of San Antonio since HemisFair. San Antonio went from being this "city that shot itself in the foot," from the perspective of the national press, to this very progressive place with this incredible young leader who's welded everybody together. And that was a fact. That's what was happening.

So companies came. Did he get them all? No. But were they excited about, you know, being around a guy like that? Sure.

Thomas Berg: *The Energy Crisis*

As chairman of City Public Service Board, Tom Berg was involved in the utility rate upheaval that began in 1974.

City Public Service Board Chairman Tom Berg.

I came to San Antonio in 1967. I had been president of a large division with Air Reduction Co. in New York City. A friend of mine was in Houston and was acquiring Freidrich Refrigeration Co. here, and asked me to come down to be the president of what they thought was a good company that had a good product, though it was failing financially and had to be saved from bankruptcy. It was my job to do that. I built that 500,000-square-foot plant on Interstate 35 in 1971.

Of course I was aware of what HemisFair was doing, because at that time Mayor Walter McAllister, whom I had met, took me over to see HemisFair being built, and the Tower of the Americans was being constructed. The top part of the tower was not complete; they just had some of the structure up there. He said, "Well, come on, let's go up there and see what it's like." I said, "Well, where's the elevator?" He said, "Oh, we're going to walk."

That's over 600 feet high, and Mayor McAllister, in his 70s, walked faster than me, and I was a lot younger. We walked all the way to the top and we walked all the way to the bottom. I was pretty well taken by that man's energy.

We went over then and I met Mr. H. B. Zachry, who was head of the group that built HemisFair, which was in deep, deep trouble. He was there to straighten out the organization and get it built on time. The first thing I was told was, "I've got your name down here for $10,000. We'd like to have the check today." That was how I was introduced to him. I called our headquarters in Houston and got approval and I gave him his $10,000.

One day I got a call from John Gatti, who was then the mayor of San Antonio. He asked me to join the City Public Service Board, which I knew nothing about.

I asked what they did and he told me, "Well, you know, it's a very routine thing; there's nothing much going on in the city with troubles, so you'll enjoy it very much, and the mighty fine people." I was to take the place of the retiring president of Joske's. At that time Jack Locke was the chairman, and he was going to retire a year later. I joined the board, I believe it was 1972 or '73, and was later elected the chairman of the board in February of 1973 or '74.

There was nothing going on until I got elected chairman. Suddenly there was a shortage of natural gas for heating and generating electricity. This was a pipeline business that Costal States, through its Lovaca Gathering Co., was supposed to deliver to the city of San Antonio under a 30-year contract of fixed prices.

The shortage occurred almost overnight because of the horrible 1972–73 war between Israel and the Arabs. And the oil and gas shortage and gasoline lines for your cars was pretty serious. With the war we had gasoline rationing, higher prices and short supplies, and most of all the problems that come with that, because most of the gas that we were getting in Texas was going out east by the biggest pipeline at higher prices. So they were getting our gas.

The contract price called for starting at 19 cents to 20 cents a thousand cubic feet. I believe each four or five years it was supposed to go up another penny. But overnight, the Texas Railroad Commission mandated that all gas companies in which Coastal/Lovaca was involved could pass along their cost to their customers, in effect saying contracts are no longer valid. Overnight the cost went from 30 cents, 40 cents, before you knew to a dollar per thousand cubic feet.

Being a city operation, we had no way to absorb these very high costs, so we were passing them along to customers. This caused very high gas and electric bills. When you used to pay $50 a month, suddenly you're paying $100 and $125 a month. Suddenly, some people were paying as much for the utility bills as they were for their rent.

The public and press simply enjoyed blaming City Public Service, and we had nothing to do with it. All we could do was either refuse to pay for it, which meant we wouldn't get the gas, which meant we'd have no gas for heat and electricity, or we had to pay the bill. So we were between a rock and a hard place. So we had gone to oil as fast as we could, but oil's not cheap, a lot more expensive than gas and we did not have the storage facilities. We had to build storage tanks very fast.

At that time, Charlie Becker was mayor, and he would come to our meetings. I introduced a motion that CPS sue Coastal States and Lovaca, now called Valero, for contract failure. I went to Austin and talked many times to the Texas Railroad Commission chairman to get a compromise on this 100 percent cost pass-through, but he said there would be no gas if we did not take that pass-through cost. The pipeline people would shut the pipelines down, the wells would go down, or they would send the gas up East where they were getting much higher prices.

So we started a lawsuit in, I believe, 1974. It took about 10 years for the lawsuit to finally be settled. That's when people began to see credits on their utility bills, monthly credits, something on the order of $200 million; the gas companies paid CPS that money, and we in turn gave it to the customers right away.

Another thing I insisted on was that Lovaca Gas Gathering move its offices from Houston to San Antonio. The bankruptcy court in Austin agreed, as did the executives of Lovaca. At that time Bill Greehey, who'd been vice-president of Coastal, became president of Lovaca Gathering and all the parties accepted my proposal of Lovaca moving to San Antonio, where it became Valero, a very good citizen, and a company of over 1,500 new jobs created immediately.

Until then, we had a citizens' uproar. Many people started coming to our meetings who never did before. We had no large room to accommodate these crowds. There might have had 8 to 10 to 12 people at most of our meetings, and suddenly we had 40 and 50 and 60 people. So we moved to the top floor of the CPS building and built an air-conditioned meeting room to handle large crowds.

This was also the period when there was an air of hysteria that we've got to build a nuclear plant; if you were not building a nuclear plant you were not in the top industrial age. Many of us were not so sure that was the right thing to do; initially I was one or two of the board members against it.

At that time Tom Deely was general manager, and they were making proposals for us to have a nuclear plant. I had a very good friend who was the general manager of the nuclear power facility that takes care of Chicago. He told me the problem was fuel, that the government is supposed to take the spent fuel off of their hands but still didn't know what to do with it, and was causing a major problem. So that's what I reported. They've spent hundreds of millions of dollars trying to figure out what to do and still don't know. And the South Texas Nuclear Project wound up costing many more times than estimated.

Clifford Morton: *Water and Politics*

Cliff Morton was a builder and developer on City Council in 1973–75 and chairman of the San Antonio Water System from 1992 to 1996.

I think that HemisFair was a turning point for this city. With HemisFair came what I would call the emergence of the first group of new entrepreneurs. Prior to World War II—I was not here then—this town was controlled by people who, generally speaking, had been here for a long, long time, the old money.

After the war you had new entrepreneurs—Ray Ellison, Quincy Lee, Jimmy Burke, Edgar Von Scheel, McCreless, we could go on and on, not just in homebuilding but in other fields. This was the first group of entrepreneurs to influence the development of the city.

With HemisFair came some new people. At the same time, you had old companies who were owned locally—Joske's, Frost's, the local banks. That began to change as we started to bring in corporations publicly owned outside the city. San Antonio has always had an identity question as to what it wanted to be. Until the census of 1930, San Antonio was the largest city in Texas, older than Houston or Dallas but always seeming to aspire to be that way. Yet there was also a conflict that said no, we want to leave things like they have been.

HemisFair was a turning point. Its legacy is the physical infrastructure and improvements left as the foundation for what is now one of our largest industries, conventions and tourism, hospitality. What to do with the rest of the land was a key argument when I was on City Council. HemisFair started to change the city's attitude about itself, that we can be different from other cities and still have a good self-esteem. There are times I wonder about our self-esteem because we tend to make financial or economic comparisons to Houston or Dallas.

I think there are other ways to compare a city than with statistics. Would I want to live there? Many of my friends made career sacrifices coming here, perhaps reluctantly, never having been here before, then fell in love with the city and are willing to not accept promotions just because they like to live in this city.

Homebuilder Clifford Morton.

A number of things happened during the late 1970s and '80s. First, you start with people in the development business, normally risk takers, entrepreneurs. Many think that just because they can build one type of product, a house, and are expert at that, they can transfer that expertise to building an office building. I had that experience in Dallas in the mid- to late '80s. That was a very costly experience for me, to find out how little I knew about something that was construction but didn't have the expertise I needed.

But you had lenders, who, under laws changed in the late '70s and early '80s to distort the financial condition in a more positive way, created an environment to where they were pushing money out the front door to people who were not qualified to develop projects. You became a partner with them, and if you were warm and said you were a developer, there were some who said, "OK, we will loan you this money, and we'll loan you enough money to where you not only don't have to put any equity in the project, we're going to charge you four points on the front end and we're going to book that as profit." So they were overstating their financial position.

After Congress found what was happening, it shut the supply of money off and aggravated the situation even more. That was a catastrophe. There was land-flipping going on in those days, inflating prices,

fueled by easy access to money from some savings and loans by individual not qualified to take that money and use it properly. There was
such optimism that reality was completely lost in the process.

One thing that hasn't changed since I came here is that San Antonio still does not have any supplemental water. It's similar to having
only one supplier of gas. We were totally dependent on natural gas to
fire our generating plants, and reserves supposed to back up that sole
contract were not there.

It was the end of the ability of a one-wage earner to buy a starter
house, and it flipped in a two-year period. In 1973, 80 percent of our
buyers were one-income households. Two years later, 80 percent were
two-income households. And you had electric rates that went through
the roof and the start of runaway inflation.

Water Resources Are Not Inexhaustible

Back to water. Let's start with San Angelo. In the drought of the
'50s they had to bring water in railroad tank cars. We have never experienced that kind of shortage in San Antonio. There is a big difference
between people's ability to go out and look at the level of a reservoir,
or fly over several reservoirs, as opposed to their ability to understand
that there are limitations on a natural resource, where you're largest
city in the United States that depends solely on underground water.

Some citizens have the ability to convince a majority that this is an
inexhaustible resource because you can't see how much is in it. It's not
a question of how much is in it, it's how much you can take out and still
respect the rights of others who also have a need for this resource.

But we have the problem: number one, you can't see it; number
two, the perception we were here first, we're the biggest and theoreti-
cally we could pump everyone else dry. The attitude has been with
some that we'll take all we want and whatever is left for people to the
east and west, that's what they'll get, which has brought enmity from
farmers from the west and recreational users to the east, in New
Braunfels and San Marcos, also from industrial users downstream.

What we have to do is to look at this first, as we do have a unique
natural resource. I have no question that it has more capacity to hold
water than all the surface water reservoirs in the state of Texas combined. But you cannot rely on a given quantity of rainfall over a certain

period of time. If you look back over the past 20 years versus the past 200 years, we're in a very wet period relative to where we have been.

What we need to do is establish a historical right to being able to pump a quantifiable quantity of water out of the Edwards Aquifer, establish the benchmark and say that from here we have to conserve water and create a water market so we can lease water rights on a short- or long-term, drought management basis for one year if we want to.

We are now pumping or discharging approximately 50,000 acre feet per day, which no one downstream has claims on, into the Gulf of Mexico. It could certainly be put to a better and higher use in golf courses, cemeteries, industrial parks, recreational parks. I think we might well see a day when we have dual lanes where even landscaping for single-family lots might be irrigated with what's called "gray water."

My biggest disappointments during my tenure at SAWS were the defeats of the Applewhite reservoir as a long-term water supply for this community. I think we lost the best and cheapest opportunity we'll ever have. Forty million dollars that was invested by this community in that project is not even a minimum down payment on what it will ultimately cost this community as we start to develop alternate resources.

How's the city different since 1968 in other areas? When I was on the council, the buildup of resentment of neglect of the south and west was about to the explosion point. I did not know Mayor Charlie Becker until a few months before I was elected. We probably disagree more than any two people in town, yet he's one of my very best friends. But he had a way about him, even though he came from what people from the south and west and east sides of town would say is the privileged class—North Side, Cavaliers, Country Club. He had a feeling about the average citizen I think he conveyed during his tenure. I think he recognized that this pressure had built up to the point where, as he used to say, you had to "open up the front doors to City Hall to everybody."

I can remember how frustrated and impatient I would get. I was 40 years old at the time, when citizens to be heard might last two hours, everybody got to talk, most of them the same folks, but letting off steam was important. He seemed to me to convey to people that he was really interested in the condition of the less fortunate.

I wish he were given credit for what I think was a very important role in the transition from the Good Government League to loss of control by the Good Government League, and from that to districting. I think redistricting changed the perception of the way less privileged sectors viewed city government. It was done very gracefully and not piecemeal. Even though on a per capita basis we're not as rich as some other cities in Texas, I think we are light years ahead of either Houston or Dallas, and, for that matter, Austin, in having a community that works well together, especially considering our diversity.

I think the fear that members of City Council would be concerned about their districts and that only the mayor could have the big picture of what was going on was overstated. Sure, there're probably many examples of where, on a particular issue, a councilperson might have abused that or confirmed that fear. But if you're going to succeed and be successful for your district, as well as the city as a whole, you'll always have to remember that it takes six votes. And if you understand that, then all of a sudden you have to be interested in the whole city.

I was actively opposed to complete districting. I was concerned that you really only had one city councilperson for the whole city, and that was the mayor, and you had ten district votes. But I look at Frank Wing, from the South Side. He was concerned for the city as a whole. If I were trying to select the councilperson I think was most effective over all those years, I would say Frank Wing was the most effective of any. He knew how to get six votes better than anybody I've ever met.

Henry and Mary Ann Noonan Guerra:
A Mixture of Cultures

In 1939 civic leader Henry Guerra, at the age of 21, became the first Mexican American newscaster on a major English-language radio station, a record he repeated in television when WOAI-TV went on the air ten years later. His wife, Mary Ann, has written several books on San Antonio's history.

Henry: I started with WOAI as a radio broadcaster, both announcer and newsman back in 1939, so I've been around quite some time. I was born here, baptized at the cathedral, went into the Army during 1942 to 1945 and have been here ever since. Mostly I've been in broadcasting with WOAI and WOAI-TV.

I did work for HemisFair. It really brought this town to life. The downtown river had been fixed up some years before with a WPA labor project, but you didn't dare go down there at night. Ever since HemisFair and development of the river as a commercial success, tourism has really taken off.

Mary Ann Noonan Guerra and Henry Guerra.

Mary Ann: I was born in Hondo, where my father was county judge. I think HemisFair was probably the most important event in our history to highlight this place. We had beautiful natural resources; we had the river, the missions, the Alamo, but we had to bring people here to let them see them. I think this was the greatest advertising piece we ever did because we sold San Antonio.

Also, it brought the Federal Building and the Institute of Texan Cultures, with its library that's a center for research. With its exhibits the institute has provided an education for so many of our children from all over the state. For them to come and see what their great-grandparents did makes them not only feel a part of the state, but educates them as to what their people did and the contributions they made. I honestly don't know what would have happened to the city if we hadn't had HemisFair.

We married in 1955, a Noonan marrying a Guerra. Henry was a well-known Hispanic famous for television and radio, but in my little home town I did not encounter any discrimination. In fact, I think I became sort of a heroine because it was like I was bringing home a movie star. It was all over the papers; I would go down the street and everyone was so delighted.

Henry: The real prejudice at that time was against the blacks. Some legal discrimination had been done away with earlier by various laws, and there were always a few prominent Hispanics in the Legislature, even some Texas Rangers. Throughout the history of this town you'll find prejudice, but you also find prominent, wealthy Hispanics—they had to be wealthy—who were not discriminated against as badly as blacks were. Nonetheless, there was the same kind of discrimination you find south of the border, economic discrimination, where the rich feel superior to the poor. The poor are not going to join the country club; they can't afford it. But there should be no legal barriers, no educational barriers to prevent the poor from bettering their situation.

Mary Ann: This is where World War II made the real leap forward, for the Mexicans who came back from World War II had open to them a subsidized education, and some of our finest attorneys and some of our finest judges and the doctors are products of that.

Henry: Kelly Field is a prime example. Because most men had gone off to war, they found they could put women in there and found that Hispanics could be taught to repair propellers, repair aircraft, and so forth. The wage level for the Hispanics, especially, came up; all the wage levels in San Antonio came up because of the federal payroll.

We're a success story here in San Antonio of the progress that has been made for different ethnic groups to like each other. Now, it has to be taught, carefully taught, at home, and, unfortunately, many of the younger generation don't get this benefit of this kind of teaching. But the fact is if you compare today with, say, the 1930s, there is far less prejudice against even the poor Mexicano than there was then.

When I was growing up in the 1920s, City Hall was controlled by the old city machine. We had a mayor and four commissioners. If you knew the right people you could pick up the phone and get the hole in your street fixed up. That no longer obtains. You can know the mayor and it's no guarantee you're gonna get your street fixed. But in those days we had paper ballots, and they used to open up the ballot boxes and they could tell how you had voted.

Local government now is much more open and responsive, but I think we have too many single-member districts. If you have 11 or 12 members on a City Council you've got a big debating society. You're not as efficient as you were when a dictator ran things at City Hall.

Election of Henry Cisneros as mayor was a watershed, yet historically it is not correct to say he was the first modern Hispanic elected mayor. What do you think Bryan Callaghan was? Bryan Callaghan was married to a Canary Islander and his mother was a Canary Islander. The first Bryan Callaghan must have been in the 1850s or so, the second Bryan Callaghan toward the 1880s, 1890s.

Mary Ann: About the role of women, I belonged to the League of Women Voters and also the Conservation Society in the work they were doing. I think it's been remarkable what has gone on in San Antonio without any real dust-ups, because the women are very powerful here. The river, the Alamo and the missions were all saved by women who had to convince their husbands to back them up.

Henry: One of the changes I've seen is in economics. It used to be that the geography of San Antonio worked against it. A legend is that the city fathers and the city owners or businesses kept the Ford Motor Co. out. If the Ford Motor Co. really wanted to come in here, they'd come in here. But why would they come here? The raw materials are miles away and you have to develop a force that's educated to do that kind of work at the time. It was our location that worked against us. We were too far from the markets they wanted, too far from the raw materials, and the freight differential kept San Antonio down.

I do want to say this: My wife, when I first met her and was courting her and even after we got married, worked for Frost Bros., which had their big store downtown. Downtown Houston and Commerce streets used to be the commercial center of San Antonio. In the 1920s everybody went to the movies downtown and went to see Broadway shows that came downtown.

We lost all that from about the late '60s, and gradually you saw a death of the retail business downtown. We're trying to change that by redoing downtown and getting people living downtown. We have to get not just rich people; we have to provide walk-ups or apartments like New York and other big cities do for the ordinary person.

Mary Ann: John Connally was governor and saw the photographs taken for the local exhibit at the Institute of Texan Cultures. Among them were the typical Mexican scenes, what everybody thought of as the fellow with the big sombrero and the baggy pants and all. He called down and said, "Change it. I want it brought up to date."

They brought in Black Star and Black Star hired me to go around with the photographer to take photographs of people like Doctor Urrutia, who was head of the surgery at Santa Rosa. We had pilots out at Randolph Field, we had Albert Pena, we had all of these people that were involved in politics, in medicine, in education, and we shot all these photographs. I have no idea who did the first set of photographs, but Connally came in and he liked the second, and that's how we got a better view of San Antonio. But that shows you how whoever worked on the first draft of photographs thought of Mexicans.

Henry: I'll tell you a personal story. Mary and I knew a young lady who was the daughter of a prominent developer who developed a big section of the city and made a lot of money, and because of the daughter we'd go to some of the parties he threw. I was standing in the mansion holding a glass of good scotch when he started in on the Mexicans, and I finally said, "Well, Mr. So and So, you've got to remember one thing. I'm a Mexican." And you know what he said to me? He said, "Well, I don't mean your kind of Mexican."

San Antonio is unique. It has a mixture of many cultures running all through its history. We've had prejudice in this town, we still do, but I think we are less prejudiced than many other towns because we know more of our history. We learn to appreciate the other guy, and our future is bright because we are getting the light industries.

We need to provide the payrolls. You can't be much of a good fellow if you're worried about putting meat on the table. We've got to improve the economy of San Antonio, we've got to improve the understanding of San Antonio and, most of all, we have to improve the educational opportunities we provide for all of our children.

Henry E. Catto Jr.: *A Changed City*

Henry Catto left San Antonio in 1969 to begin a government career that included posts as U.S. Chief of Protocol at the White House, Assistant Secretary of Defense for Public Affairs, U.S. Ambassador to Great Britain and director of the U.S. Information Agency. He returned in 1993 to live in a much-changed San Antonio.

To look at San Antonio's enormous political, economic and social changes between the time I left in 1969 and my return in 1993, let's start with the political.

I was involved with the founding of the modern Texas Republican Party. I was part of a ticket that ran in 1960, the first time Republicans had fielded a broad-based ticket for the Texas Legislature. Those of us

who studied political science in college came away thinking that you ought to have competing parties, not endless internecine warfare within a single party. This began as a bit of an intellectual enterprise and turned into a serious political movement.

Those of us who ran the first time in 1960, including Ike Kampman for the Senate and four of us for the House of Representatives, all got shot down, but not disastrously. We managed somehow or another to garner 45 percent of the vote, most of us. Which was no disgrace, given the background of the time.

Former Ambassador Henry Catto Jr.

And now I come back to a San Antonio, almost a quarter of a century later, where the county judge is a Republican! Unthinkable! The only county office we were able to capture back in my days when I was very active was Precinct 3 county commissioner, which included the heart districts of Republican strength in northeastern Bexar County.

Now not only do we have the county judge but we've had a county commissioner and two Republican congressmen in this area—and a sheriff, of all things. It's just simply amazing. And district judges; who ever thought that there'd be a Republican judge? Certainly, I wouldn't have. But it has so turned out.

As for the economics of San Antonio, I remember very well when La Quinta Motor Inns went public and got listed on the New York Stock Exchange. It was unheard of. It was maybe 1965 or '66. It was exciting for the young business people around town that this was the home office of a stock exchange–listed company. Of course, the banks had always been publicly owned. But the business community in San Antonio was pretty much old guard, very minor league. I came back and was thunderstruck to see that there were dozens of companies headquartered here that are publicly owned and listed on the New York, American or NASDAQ stock exchanges.

I was driving over the George Washington Bridge in Washington, D.C., on my way home one day, when I heard on National Public Radio that Southwestern Bell was leaving St. Louis and coming to San Antonio. I almost drove into the Potomac River. I just couldn't believe that that would happen, and yet it did. It's an amazing change!

In downtown San Antonio, the greatest change is that there are people downtown. Twenty-four years ago we had begun to see the wilting of Houston Street as a main commercial thoroughfare. And, of course, that got worse and worse and worse until it became a bunch of blindeyes looking out on no traffic. Just walking over here from my office I was amazed at how many people there are downtown. This, of course, is a result of what's happened on the river.

I remember a guy from Houston, a developer who came over here, a fellow I knew slightly. He said, "You know, what you really ought to do is develop the river and connect it to the Alamo." I remembered his comments when I walked through the lobby of the Hyatt Hotel and saw, indeed, that there is now a direct path between the Alamo and the river, a very nice one to walk on.

Retail downtown has blossomed with creation of River Center Mall. And there's retail on the river itself. The convention and visitor industry is extraordinary. The business leadership and political leadership, first of all, pulled together enough to create HemisFair itself. That was an unheard of thing.

Slipping over into social changes, until HemisFair came along Jessica and I didn't know a single Latino in San Antonio. We were ghettoized with strictly our Anglo friends. HemisFair changed all that. All of a sudden we were working with, and getting to know, a lot of Latino people. That has made a big difference, not only in the architectural and structual situation downtown, but in the social situation.

I haven't seen the Medical Center from the inside. But I've been to a doctor's office out there, and was just astonished at the size of it. None of that was there except maybe the Methodist Hospital.

Speaking of educational facilities, to look at the way Trinity has grown and to see the overnight—or at least so it seems to Rip Van Winkle here—emergence of the University of Texas at San Antonio as a big, really good university is astonishing.

San Antonio is so much better. It's more interesting. I've brought a lot of out-of-towners here to visit the class I teach at UTSA and taken them around, doing a little touring to reward them for coming and taking the trouble to visit the class. I've been amazed at how interesting San Antonio is. For instance, well, two for-instances. Tourist assets have grown exponentially. There was nothing like Sea World or Fiesta Texas. There's now an astonishingly handsome resort hotel, the Hyatt, out on the northwest side. Beautifully done. We never had a destination resort like that.

Furthermore, we never had anything like the road complex that now serves the city. I remember the great battle when Mayor Walter McAllister was trying to force through construction of US 281 North, what we used to call the North Expressway. A lot of people were against it—it would ruin Olmos Park and so on and so forth. It didn't harm them a bit, but what it did do was provide rapid transportation, north and south. And now you can do it north, south, east and west, and with two loops to boot, you can really move around. I got so used to being in parking lots when we lived in Washington, where you just have to wait and wait and wait in traffic jams. That doesn't often happen here. The great old tourist attractions—the missions and the Governor's Palace and the Alamo and that sort of thing—are still beautifully maintained and moving and interesting. And the people come by the carload lot.

Another thing that strikes me, because I like to eat, is how many really good restaurants there are in San Antonio. Back when we left there was La Louisiane and the Argyle Club and that was about it. Now you can't stir them with a stick; you've got to flip a coin to pick which really good restaurant you want to go to.

Also, there has certainly been more interest in what's going on beyond our borders. And, to a certain extent, more respect for Mexico and less of the sort of "Perotista," that is to say the Ross Perot kind of anti-Mexicanism that was fairly typical when I left. On the other hand, I'm not sure that the so-called aristocracy of the city has learned all that much, as a whole. I think you still find people pretty close-minded.

I don't think I've ever seen a black person at the San Antonio Country Club, for example. Other than as a waiter, of course.

That may be changing. I noticed that a black couple was invited to join another eating club, the Club Giraud, downtown, but not without a battle, apparently. I heard one of the old-line stuffy members chewing out a board member at a Christmas party, just giving him unshirted hell for having voted to admit a black couple into this club—which is a club, after all, for the benefit of the Southwest Craft Center. There ought to be no question but what it should be open to anybody who is compatible and attractive and can afford it, and clearly there are plenty of blacks who can afford it.

Back when we left town there were three papers: the *Express*, the *News* and the *Light*. It's sad to see the forces of the market and the innovations in electronic media cut the number of newspapers down, because, for me, the heart of the news business is the newspaper. That may be a dated idea, but that's the way I feel. And there were five television stations: the three networks, KLRN, and Channel 41, broadcasting in Spanish on KWEX. Now, of course, with cable, that's a big change. I'm not sure that it's a whole lot better, but it's different.

As long as we're talking electronic, one of the wonderful changes is in radio, because when I left, and long after I left, San Antonio had no public radio. Then a classical music station began on a string, and it was really terribly amateurishly done by people who love it but didn't know much about the medium.

And now, of course, we have a National Public Radio station and Trinity and the classical station. Just tremendous improvements from the wasteland of commercial radio.

I've been amazed at the flowering of nontraditional churches in San Antonio like Cornerstone Church out on 1604 which I ran across on television. There's another one I saw out on I-35 going south, there off to the east—a big, big new church. Nice little ole places like where I grew up, at First Presbyterian or St. Mark's or Christ Church, or what-have-you, are sort of eclipsed, at least in numbers, I suspect, by these vast, new, sort of independent pentacostal churches.

The presence of the Catholic church, of course, is still major here, and I guess always will be. Wonder how long it will be before we get a cardinal from San Antonio?

Appendix: Two Other Evolutions

Even as HemisFair was winding down, another hard-fought-for change was occurring: establishment of a medical school in San Antonio, which would also soon lose its unenviable place as the state's only major city without a publicly funded university.

Then there was an upheaval in control of San Antonio's daily newspapers, the traditional forum for local communication and debate, which played out quite differently from most daily newspaper wars elsewhere.

The Medical School

Blair Reeves: *The Crucial Vote*

Blair Reeves served as Bexar County Judge for more than 11 years. He later was elected a County Court-at-Law judge and then to the Fourth Court of Civil Appeals, of which he served as chief justice.

I've lived in San Antonio all my life, except for the time that I was in the Marine Corps. I got hit on Okinawa on May 20, 1945, took fire from an automatic weapon. That's when I got into a wheelchair. I was in a Navy hospital for about two years.

When I came back to San Antonio I enrolled at San Antonio College, met my wife, Betty, went to Baylor for my first year of law school, then transferred here to San Antonio and went to St. Mary's. They had a two-way communications system. I sat over in the corner of the library with earphones and would listen to the classroom discussion and the lecture.

I'd take all my examinations in that corner of the library. I finished up in law school that way in 1951.

I knew no politicians and didn't know anybody to go to work for, so I started a little practice just out on West Avenue. I found out the Justice of the Peace out there was making $250 or $300 a month. They were only meeting about two hours a week. He was a barber named Tony Anthony. So I filed in the Democratic Primary against him for JP of Precinct 8.

I remember him coming in and telling me, "Son, why do you want to be JP?" I said, "Well, it's a good job. I don't have anything against you, Judge, but I'd like to have that job."

So he said, "Well, you'll never be able to make those inquests—you're in a wheelchair." I said, "Yeah, I can do that." He said, "Well, hold off for two years and I'll give it to you. I got other plans." I think he wanted to run for county commissioner. I remember just specifically saying, "Judge, that job's not yours to give."

He said, "Well, I'm going to beat you." And I said,

County Judge Blair Reeves presided from a wheelchair.

"Yeah, you might, but bring your lunch, it's going to be an all-day job." So anyway, here I was a disabled veteran in a dadgum wheelchair and a local guy. I beat poor Tony like a drum. I got over 1,800 votes, and he got about five.

I took office January 1, 1953. I held that job for six years. In one year, I made 52 or 53 inquests. In my little precinct I don't think there were 5 or 10 deaths during that year, but a JP could go all over the county, and these other guys quite often weren't available. The San Antonio Police Department always knew that I answered my phone, and they'd always call me, and I always got the SAPD's support every time I ran for election.

After six years on the job I was tired and left it. My law practice was coming along. I was over there with John Daniels. I ran for county chairman of the Democratic Party against Jimmy Knight in 1960. Burt

Thompson, later bankruptcy judge, ran for the county chairman's job too. Jimmy Knight beat me like a drum. He beat Burt and me without a runoff, just really tromped me. It was a very humbling experience. I went back to practicing law, and in '66 ran for county judge, and won.

I served over eleven years as county judge. One of my big moments came on the vote that established the county hospital as a teaching hospital so we could get a medical school here. Prior to 1966, the Legislature passed this law which would allow Bexar County to tax the people of the county with a hospital district tax and gave the option to allow them to assess it at a larger amount. If you had a $10,000 home it would be on the tax rolls at $2,500. We assessed property at 25 percent of market value at that time, and then it fluctuated from year to year. If the voters of Bexar County voted for this referendum they could raise that assessment to 50 percent of market value.

The election was to be held January 17, 1967. At that time the teaching hospital of Bexar County, out there at the medical complex, was about 50 or 60 percent complete. The medical school was about the same way. The people of Bexar County had voted a bond issue of $5 million for the building of a new county hospital.

The county government took that $5 million and went to the federal government and got $10 million, what they call Hill-Burton Funds, because at that time we needed new hospitals in the United States and more medicine, more doctors and things of that nature. That was the incentive. We'd spent our bond money and we were using these Hill-Burton Funds. But in January 1967, the people voted no. And here we had no way in God's world to open that hospital.

Frank Erwin was chairman of the University of Texas Board of Regents, a very persuasive, very volatile, tough guy. He said we needed to do something about this hospital. "How are you going to fund this hospital? How are you going to open the doors? Are you going to get it completed? How are you going to open the doors if you don't have the money to operate the staff or to buy the supplies or anything of this nature? And you've got to find a way." I said, "I don't know how we're going to do it, Mr. Erwin, but, anyway, the people have said no."

So he finally asked me to call the Commissioners Court. On the court at that time were Albert Peña, Ollie Wurzbach, Jim Helland, A. J. Ploch, and I was county judge. This was before open meetings and all.

Commissioners Court met with John Peace and Frank Erwin. John Peace was on the Board of Regents at the University of Texas, and later was chairman. So helpful. So we got up in this suite in the Gunter Hotel and ate lunch, and then Frank Erwin posed the question to me: "What are you going to do about funding that hospital?" And I said, "Well, we don't know. The people turned it down."

So he said, "Let me tell you, Judge, what I'm going to do. I want a plan on how you're going to raise the money to operate that hospital. Because I'm going to tell you what. Iif you don't do this, I'm going to take that school, my building over there, and I'm going to make a nursing school out of it or I'm going to make a dental school out of it." He said, "My school."

He said, "You're going to have that hospital over there and the federal government is going to start asking you for funds, and you ain't going to be able to pay those funds, and you've got $5 million worth of your own money in there and then you owe the federal government some money. I don't know what in the hell you're going to do, but it's going to be an unfinished edifice to your administration."

He left and I said, "What are we going to do, you guys?" And they all looked at each other, and then the Chamber of Commerce started having meetings, and the *Express* started having editorials: "Something needs to be done; let's make some decisions." I remember meeting with Bob Rolf, president of the Chamber of Commerce, and Pat Zachry, Walter McAllister, John Peace. And they said, "Well, Judge, what are you going to do?"

I don't know if it was Frank Erwin or who came up with the suggestion: Go back to the Legislature and we'll ask the Legislature to give the Commissioners Court the option to double the tax. Then we'll get our hospital and we'll get it going. I said, "What in the hell are you talking about? The people have spoken, Mr. Erwin." And he said, "Well, give me an answer, give me an alternative." I remember Mr. Zachry coming up to me and saying, "Judge, what are you going to do? You've got to do something."

I went home that night, and I said, "You know, Betty, you've heard that expression 'Somebody needs to do something about that, something ought to do something about this.' Well, that someone is me."

I called Mr. Erwin and said, "I polled my group." And I did, I asked the commissioners, individually, "What would you do about, what do you think about doubling the tax?" Albert Peña said, "Hell, no, I'm not going to do it." Ollie Wurzbach said, "I don't know." Jim Helland said, "Sure." Ploch said, "No way, buddy, no way." So I went back to Ollie, and Ollie said, "Yeah, I'll vote for it."

We got that legislation through and were on tenterhooks that somebody on the local delegation would fall out of line. But they all stayed hitched and it shot through there, and Gov. John Connally signed it. There were more and more phone calls: "Don't you vote for that thing. It's outlandish." And one thing and another. Started getting all this heat about don't raise the tax.

We sent it down for a public hearing, had it on a Saturday morning. That probate court filled up, people were standing in the aisles. All the medical faculty showed up. They had been teaching out at Trinity University and had been working at some of these hospitals like the Green.

And, boy, then the "anti's." They talked for I don't know how long. After we finally came up for the vote, everybody had said their piece, I made the motion, Helland seconded it and we started calling the roll. You call first Albert Peña, and he votes no. And then Ollie was next; he voted yea. And then Jim Helland voted yea, and Ploch voted no.

I told those people, "You know, I might be county judge for only one term, but during that term I'm going to be county judge. I think this is in the best interest of Bexar County, and I vote aye."

Jim Helland and Ollie stayed hitched and were just as important in the whole thing as I was, of course, 'cause it took three votes. But I got the brunt of the criticism. I guess it was more proper since I was county judge. But after that, the phones rang off the hook and it got so bad they threatened my life and all that stuff. One evening I just took Betty and our two kids and went down and checked into a motel, stayed there just to get out of the house.

I never lost a race after that. The interesting thing is that I ran again in '70. And in '69 a committee made up of Roy Barrera, John Peace, Bob Sawtelle, Jack Daniels, Sol Casseb, Walter McAllister Jr. and Dr. Bob Hilliard formed to raise me funds. That's a pretty broad-based committee. They got the support of the community and they filled that Villita Assembly Hall up and turned over a check to me of about $22,000. I want to say I got in the high 70 percent of the votes. Then I went over and was a County Court-at-Law judge and ran for reelection there. Then ran for the Court of Appeals and didn't get any opposition.

John Howe: *A Far-Reaching Impact*

Dr. John Howe was president of the University of Texas Health Science Center at San Antonio from 1985 to 2000.

I came to San Antonio to lead the Health Science Center family in 1985. Between the time I lifted off from Logan Airport in Boston and arrived in San Antonio, three things had fallen: 13 inches of snow, the price of oil and higher education budgets. We were faced with choices: deny reality and be sorrowful, or move ahead and develop the next phase for the Health Science Center. The latter choice was selected.

The Health Science Center today is a tremendous tribute to both campus and community. Eight hundred-plus nursing students stand in stark contrast to 1972, when the nursing school was built to house 225. This growth has largely occurred during the past decade. Today ours is the largest nursing school in the University of Texas System.

On the other side of the ledger, Jim Reed at the Heart Association put it well. In 1985 we received about $48,000 in research awards from the American Heart Association. This year that hit $975,000, just from one funding source. Overall, our research awards have grown from about $30 million a year in the mid-'80s to well over $100 million.

The significance of that lies in the dollars, but also in the fact that most of these monies come through peer review, a competitive process, which speaks well for the effectiveness of our faculty here at the Health Science Center. So there are many indices from students' research that can, in a way, serve as proof pudding of the changes that occurred in this past decade. We now have the Health Science Center, numerous private hospitals, University Hospital, Bexar County Hospital and the Veteran's Administration Hospital, plus clinics, practices, everything. Where once cows were pastured are 22,000 people.

There's a wonderful story associated with the beginning of the Medical School. In 1946, a group of San Antonians trekked up to Austin and visited the Legislature. Their intent was to demonstrate that San Antonio was the largest city in the U.S. without a medical school, and now was the time to fix that. In the stealth of the night they became very, very close to succeeding in bringing that medical school to San Antonio. The way they did it was unusual. They came within two votes in the Texas Senate of creating the legal language that would move the Medical Branch on Galveston Island to San Antonio.

Needless to say, when that was discovered at daybreak it caused great consternation at the Capitol, particularly among those who cared deeply about Galveston Island.

So it wasn't an accident that not much was heard from the Legislature for many years having to do with a medical school in San Antonio. I'm told that whenever San Antonio came forth, there were people checking their pockets to make sure there wasn't a loose medical school around that the San Antonians might take home.

Dr. John Howe, Health Science Center president for 15 years.

It was in the late '50s that the city was successful. And again, a wonderful story. One of our community leaders, at that point in time, was none other than C. C. "Pop" Gunn. He happened to have great influence, but additionally he was president of the Texas Automobile Dealers' Association that year. He said, "I think this is the year."

With the coming together of a number of people in this community, very notably Dr. John Smith, they trekked up to Austin again. But this time they had a very special ally: the lobbyist for the Texas Automobile Dealers' Association, who Pop enlisted in this cause. That lobbyist was very, very effective in getting the Legislature to agree to the medical school. He worked the floors of the House and Senate to make that happen. Ultimately, we were chartered in 1959 by the Legislature not as the UT Health Science Center of San Antonio, but as the South Texas Medical School. That lobbyist became lieutenant governor of the State of Texas, Bob Bullock. So there is no question that Bob Bullock had a keen interest in what he referred to as "his" medical school.

The first class of students was around 1970. But the construction of the campus was in 1966, '67, '68. Wonderful pictures from the top of Methodist Hospital look across the way, with a couple of silos, with a sign that said "Future Home of South Texas Medical School."

Methodist Hospital was out there by itself. There was a question as to whether it would be successful in developing a medical complex, given the distance. But now there are 22,000 people who work every day there. Our biggest problem is not delivery of health care; it is delivery of employees, getting people in and out of the Medical Center.

The South Texas Medical Center, the tract now numbering about 800 acres, is governed by the San Antonio Medical Foundation. That board has been a tremendous advocate for the Medical Center in general and the Medical School in particular. On the campus is the land given to the Health Science Center and to the board of regents. That's 100 acres. We subsequently have an additional acreage down the street for the building given to us with monies from Ross Perot.

The parent campus is about 100 acres and allows us a very real presence in academic medicine here in the U.S. It's an academic health center with a Medical School; Nursing School; Dental School; School of Allied Health Sciences; a graduate School of Biomedical Sciences; in partnership with UT Austin, a College of Pharmacy; and, in partnership with the Health Science Center at Houston, a School of Public Health. Seven professional schools. All told, we have just under 3,000 students, interns and residents being educated at this institution every day by full-time and part-time, about 1,300 faculty members.

Physically connected with the Health Science Center is University Hospital, a 600-bed teaching hospital well known for trauma services and transplantation services and its one-of-a-kind neonatology unit. Physically attached to University Hospital is the Audie Murphy Veterans Hospital, also about 600 beds, serving the region called South Texas.

Just across the street is the first facility in the complex, Methodist Hospital, which has grown and grown, most recently with an 11-story tower.

Add to that 12 hospitals in the Medical Center, from St. Luke's to Regional to Women's and Children's to Villa Rosa to Santa Rosa Northwest—a vibrant medical complex. Unlike Houston, which has land at an absolute premium, we have about 250 acres yet to be developed.

Military Medicine and the Texas Research Park

Our principal military affiliations are with University Hospital, VA Hospital, Brooke Army Medical Center, and Wilford Hall Air Force Medical Center. Back in 1985 there was a tremendous debate over the future of one of our four teaching hospitals, Brooke Army Medical Center. The then Assistant Secretary of Defense thought we needed to close Brooke Army Medical Center and replace it with a station hospital, maybe 150 beds as opposed to 600 beds.

At that point, the community said, "That's not a good idea. We need to replace Brooke Army Medical Center, but with a state-of-the-art teaching hospital." So we got the new 450-bed teaching hospital at Brooke Army Medical Center at Binz-Engleman and I-35. About 60 percent of our trauma cases are cared for at University Hospital, about 20 percent at Wilford Hall, 20 percent at Brooke Army Medical Center. Three Level One trauma facilities are in different parts of the city.

The University of Texas is the anchor tenant in the 1,200-acre Texas Research Park spawned in the mid-'80s with the hope of being populated by research activities over the next decade or two.

This occurred because of the recognition that in San Antonio we had such assets in the biosciences as the Health Science Center, Wilford Hall, Brooks Air Force Base, Brooke Army Medical Center, Southwest Foundation for Biomedical Research, Southwest Research Institute, and that if we could find a way to transfer some of the discoveries occurring every day at those institutions to technology and to patentable products, this would attract scientists on one hand and create jobs on the other.

As a result the Texas Research Park has the University of Texas Institute of Biotechnology, on the highest rise. Next to it is the Institute for Drug Development and the Southwest Oncology Group facility, both parts of the Cancer Therapy Research Center, plus Research Plaza

One, Research Plaza Two—which houses young start-up companies—and the Powell Conference Center and apartment complex.

The challenge is a perceptual one. When we band together as a community to create a shopping center or mall, that's something that can be very tangible very quickly. Easy to see, easy to feel, easy to walk into, easy to see its products. When we're talking about biomedical discoveries, some take years of gestation. The creation of the mall can happen overnight, the creation of a research park takes time.

Some who looked from the windows of the Methodist Hospital across the way said, "This Medical Center is just the figment of somebody's imagination. It's a dream that won't come true." I predict that in an equal time from now, 20 or 30 years, we'll see that Research Park is just as vibrant, with just as many people working there.

We have created the Southwest Research Consortium to assure our scientific family—Southwest Foundation for Biomedical Research, the Health Science Center, Trinity, the Southwest Research Institute, UTSA—there will be opportunities for collaboration and cooperation. Practically speaking, the successes we've enjoyed won't be found in any legal document but in the laboratory. And at the Health Science Center we have very close ties to the Southwest Foundation and many of its faculty have adjunct appointments at the Health Science Center.

A number of years ago there was some hostility toward the practicing faculty at the Robert B. Green Hospital who it was thought would not put their own paying patients in what is now University Hospital and thus help fund the charitable patients. That has been resolved. Probably 40 to 50 percent of the patients at University Hospital come with some funding, a dramatic change from 10 or 15 years ago. And the University Hospital is a hospital-of-choice for many kinds of illnesses that San Antonians face. For example, for a heart transplant there's no other place to go. The Level One neonatal unit is a gem in the city.

One of the early complaints about the location of the Medical School was that it was too far from center-city people who need it. I think the answer is tremendously different from it would have been in 1985, because the hospital recognized the importance of having care in the neighborhood to obviate the need for travel across the city.

So the Board of Managers allocated monies to develop West Side, South Side, East Side clinics, so people know that if they have an illness they can see their doctor in their neighborhood. If it's a more complicated outpatient concern, then go to the Brady–Green and be dealt with there. The only patients coming all the way to the Medical Center from these far-flung sites are the patients who really need tertiary care.

Are hospitals unfairly competing, duplicating expensive services? I think it is less an issue today. First, hospitals today are at maybe 60 to 70 percent occupancy. We're working with the Medical Destination San Antonio effort to find a way to bring patients from the region and from Mexico to use that excess capacity. An alternate to paring it away is to have the beds filled by paying patients from outside the region.

Second, major hospital chains and some HMOs have moved in. Their priority is cost savings, so I think they're not going to be in the business of building additional facilities, adding additional equipment.

Funding and the Legislature

We were chartered as the South Texas Medical School. In 1972 the Regents changed our name to the UT Health Science Center of San Antonio when other schools were added, but our roots remain as a South Texas institution. This was reaffirmed by the Legislature when they voted $17 million to fund activities in the Lower Rio Grande Valley, Laredo–Del Rio–Eagle Pass area and Corpus Christi–Coastal Bend.

There's no question but what trekking to Austin every two years for 140 days over funding is a challenge. However, it's also invigorating, because every two years we have gone forth with new ideas, proposals. While the Legislature has faced fiscal constraints and has severely challenged us in some instances with budget cuts, they've done some very creative things—for example, the South Texas Border Initiative in Higher Education, in which nearly $400 million was provided to educational institutions in the region to expand physical facilities, and the South Texas Border Health Initiative.

About 84 percent of the state's budget is really out of the legislature's hands, with mandates and requirements and federal matching. Only about 16 percent of those monies are actually discretionary, and guess who makes up two-thirds of the 16 percent? Higher education. So it's no accident whenever there's a difficult time they come chasing after us. But, I have to say that the Legislature has been very good to San Antonio, very good to the Health Science Center.

When the textbooks are written on San Antonio and medicine, they'll point out that San Antonio has three large industries: military, tourism and the biosciences. If you total expenditures in the biosciences this year—including research institutions, University of Texas, the hospital systems—it's about $2 billion a year.

Unlike some industries segregated on one side of town or another, the bioscience industry is in all quadrants. We have is a clean industry, a vibrant industry, but that doesn't tell the whole story. The successes we have enjoyed in biosciences have been directly related to the kind of community confederation that has advanced these various causes.

The new Brooke Army Medical Center only happened because there was an alliance of the University of Texas, the business community, the media and our elected leaders. Ross Perot was a great contributor to expansion of the Health Science Center. Now how did that happen? Well, General McDermott, Red McCombs and Henry Cisneros gave of their time, got on an airplane and went up to visit with Mr. Perot. They asked for $10 million and he said, "Why not $15 million?"

As I have visited around the country, people ask, "How is San Antonio different?" One of the things I point out is that our successes are shared ones—there's a generally accepted feeling that the health of the economy is directly related to the health of the citizenry. That isn't Republican and Democrat, it's not university or private sector, it's not town or gown. It's community.

Duncan Wimpress: *A Raising of Sights*

Dr. Duncan Wimpress served as president of Trinity University from 1970 to 1977, when he began a 15-year tenure as president of the Southwest Foundation for Biomedical Research.

San Antonio was slower paced when I came. The first major speech I gave in San Antonio was to a meeting of the Good Government League, about 1,500 people, at the Convention Center. They introduced a fellow to make some brief remarks before I was introduced as the main speaker. This guy talked an hour and 20 minutes. It turned out to be Walter McAllister, the former mayor, and that's how I first met Walter. But that was when the Good Government League was on its way out.

We've seen a lot of activist groups formed—COPS, the Metro Alliance and others, which, I think, have been a very good thing for the city. They've gotten us away from the idea of a sleepy little southwestern town, a little Mexican village with sagebrush running down the street, which we never really were. From the image of that to a very dynamic, upfront city. I think the pace has probably been the biggest change I've seen. I think the city's leaders are aiming higher than they used to.

Dr. Duncan Wimpress.

I wasn't here for HemisFair, so I didn't see that. But I think I was seeing the end of the pre-HemisFair milieu, then the beginning of the post-HemisFair. But even in the more recent years, I think I've seen a raising of sights. I think that now people here are thinking of San Antonio in terms of becoming a major player in our country, a city of real consequence, rather than just a nice, charming place to go.

In higher education there have been a number of very dramatic changes. The establishment of UTSA, and the Health Science Center. Trinity, of course, has emerged as one of the finest small universities, certainly in the western part of the United States, even in the whole country. Incarnate Word has made some very dramatic advances, and I think St. Mary's has kept pace, and Our Lady of the Lake.

The coming of the Health Science Center made a significant impact on the Southwest Foundation for Biomedical Research, because there were adjunct professorships both ways. A lot of Health Science Center faculty did research early on as part of the foundation's work. Henry McGill, scientific director through my presidency, was head of pathology at the Health Science Center and retained his faculty rank there. Virtually all upper echelon faculty at the Southwest Foundation were also adjunct faculty members at the Health Science Center.

We brought in John Vanderberg to the foundation, the first geneticist in San Antonio. We told him to build a department, and he did a magnificent job. He brought Bennett Dike and Gene McClure from

Penn State and was instrumental in bringing Bill Stone here. Bill came to Trinity, but he came only with the agreement that he would have an adjunct appointment with the Foundation. Because of Vanderberg's early work, Barbara Bowman came to the Health Science Center's Department of Genetics over there. There are probably several dozen top-flight, world-recognized geneticists in town now, through the cooperation of the Health Science Center and the Southwest Foundation.

If I had to pick a single event that I think will make the greatest difference in the long-range future of the city, it would probably be the construction of the Alamodome. Despite all the nay-sayers, I think this is very significant as it moves San Antonio into a different level, as far as major cities in this country are concerned. In the long run will make an enormous difference to what happens in San Antonio. But that's in the future. I know the thing is hurting now. I think what's happened at the Southwest Foundation, which went through a tremendously rapid and, I think, significant expansion in the last 20 years, is important.

If I were to reform education in Bexar County, the first thing I would do is cut way back on administrative staff. We spend an enormous amount of money needlessly; 13 public school districts—or whatever we have—is a disaster because of he cost. You don't have to have 13 superintendents. On the other hand, there are problems with having one. But why hasn't someone talked about having two or three or four? You don't have to go to the extreme, either way, it seems to me.

But there are areas in which we haven't made progress. We've got an old guard still, we've got the old-line San Antonians, some of whom aren't excited about new corporate guys. It's gonna take a little while.

The Newspaper War

Charles O. Kilpatrick: *Comics Shift the Tide of Battle*

Charles Kilpatrick was San Antonio Express-News *executive editor in 1958–69 and publisher in 1969–90.*

I arrived here in 1950 from Tyler, where I was editor of the paper. I did not know San Antonio, but had decided to better myself and was offered a position on the *News*, which was an afternoon paper at that time, so I came here. What struck me immediately was that San Antonio was a very attractive place to live, very interesting, bicultural, bilingual. I had not been exposed to that before.

But I was also struck with the fact that it had a small-town outlook, very provincial, not as forward-looking as I'd expected. Certainly that was true of the *Express* and the *News* and all the other media at that time. This city had its mind set in the past. It was very conservative in a social sense, although it was politically considered the most liberal city of any consequence in Texas, as it still is today, but there were conservative politics here. Nobody who was Hispanic or black ever got married; we didn't have any pictures of brides. Minority parties and that sort of thing were not covered. They didn't die in the paper, they were buried at black funeral homes who had obituaries in the paper that they paid for, but the paper didn't recognize them.

After I stayed here for a while I discovered here was a major city, that in the 1950 census had 525,000 people but had a massive inferiority complex, had not shared in the postwar boom that Houston and Dallas had. That was true because the leadership was like that, particularly the bankers, with one or two exceptions. All the media—radio, television, newspapers—were home-owned, family-owned. The Hearst family controlled the *San Antonio Light*. The Huntress family controlled the *Express* and the *News*.

There were two TV stations at that time, family-owned, the same with radio, no chain operation here at all. That was a negative in the sense they were not very progressive, not forward-looking, didn't have capital to expand in ways they could have, or perhaps should have.

But it was good to have a local base, particularly in the retail establishment, because those stores, like Wolff and Marx and Frost and Joske's and stores of that type, participated in cultural and civic affairs and gave money to things—the symphony and the opera and the ballet, the normal worthy things.

A Corrupt Political System

The most notable thing I saw was how corrupt the political system was on the county level and on the city level—ward-heeler politics at its very worst, very little consideration given for the public good. They had bad habits like passing bond issues for something called the South Side Artery, which was never built and nobody ever knew exactly where the money went, frittered away. There was open gambling. We had one gambling place that was operating within sight of the police station.

The principal patrons were judges and policemen and political figures from City Hall and the courthouse.

If you knew the right people you could get anything done, at the courthouse, the City Hall about the level of taxes you paid, or permits, that sort of thing. Everybody on the newspaper staff found it very amusing that if you got a parking ticket that you'd have to go down and pay it. You didn't do that at all. You waited until you got 15 or 20 and

Charles Kilpatrick as Express-News publisher in 1971.

you went down and got the reporter who covered the corporation court. He would go in and have them stamped "paid" and thrown in the wastebasket, and you never had to pay it. The senior editors on the paper had little green and white metal signs they put on their dashboards which allowed them to park anywhere without getting a ticket. Policemen were not allowed to give them a ticket.

There was absolutely no confidence in the integrity of government. The first house we moved into had a chug-hole literally big enough that you could drop a small sedan into the middle of it, and have all four wheels down about maybe 12 or 14 inches deep. When it was filled up with water after a rain an unsuspecting motorist would go through there and almost tear the wheels off of his car.

I suggested to a neighbor that we should call City Hall and have them fix it. He gave me an incredulous look as if I was some sort of idiot. He said, "They don't fix holes in the street." Well, I knew he was wrong; I'd lived in cities where that had happened, had covered City

Hall. So I go down and found he was right, you couldn't get anything fixed. A year later when I moved away the hole was still there.

The votes were bought. We had the poll tax, still, in those days. They would give people $2 to $3, depending on what the going rate was, to go vote for the right person. They had ways of finding out—they were all paper ballots—whether you voted correctly.

It was a time also when the GIs coming out of World War II began to take over. They'd had four to five years, a chance to work up, and they were taking over offices in City Hall at the courthouse. Most of them turned out to be just as corrupt as everybody else.

In the mid-'50s, something called the Good Government League was organized. That was made up of primarily business leaders who knew this city would never amount to anything as long as we had a political system modeled on the principles of Hague in Jersey City or Pendergast in Kansas City or Chicago politics. They were supported by the vast majority of the people, who were fed up with paying relatively high taxes for the services that they got. They swept out the people at City Hall. Didn't touch the county.

City government stabilized and the city began a pattern of growth which enabled them to get very large bond issues passed for the first time, primarily for flood control and street improvement. The Good Government League lasted 18 years, the longest running reform movement in the United States at the time the voters finally turned on it.

We've had luck in new leadership, particularly in the last 15 or 20 years. We've seen people come in and become movers and shakers who could not have in the past. They certainly would never have been eligible for the Cavaliers or the Order of the Alamo because they were born in foreign countries or other states and came here and, through skill and leadership, directed the city's course in many different ways.

A lot of our problems have been brought on simply because we thought too small. We had the feeling you couldn't do this. Well, I think now we can see that we can do it. And if we had that spirit sooner we'd be a better city than we were.

Circulation Upheaval from a Shift in Comics

In 1950, there were three newspapers. The afternoon *News* had the largest circulation, the *Express* was a close second, and the *Light* was third. It had been that way for quite a long time, and I suppose it would have stayed that way, except one thing that happened.

When I tell what happened it will be the best argument you probably will ever hear for people not retiring when they should and staying on longer than they should. I've never talked to anybody about this. First, I can tell some things that have never been said publicly or printed.

Old Mr. Huntress, Frank Huntress, had been publisher. He was publisher for 64 years. He had worked under George Brackenridge, who owned the paper and who literally gave it away to Mr. Huntress.

Brackenridge set up a trust, which had the largest block of stock, and named Mr. Huntress the lifetime president. He had the power to appoint the members of the board. The Huntress family owned some of the stock, and then there were three other families that owned, I believe it was 27 percent of the stock. So the Huntresses had effective control.

Old Mr. Huntress was quite a student. He'd done a good job of building the *Express* to be a powerhouse paper throughout southwestern Texas. He started the *News* in 1918 to compete with the *Light*, an afternoon paper, and had made a financial success of it. Like many of us, he got old, but he stayed on and continued to make decisions.

In 1953 there came a dispute between Mr. Huntress and the newspaper syndicates that controlled the comics. At that time it was typical of metropolitan newspapers to have what they called "territory," which meant that no smaller newspaper within their territory could buy the same comics, columns and features. The *Express* territory went down as far as Corpus Christi and Brownsville, as far out into West Texas as they wanted to go, clear up, I guess, beyond Austin to Waco. That gave them the exclusive right to buy features.

That worked out all right; it was okay with the syndicate to continue that, but as those cities grew right after World War II they became bigger, particularly Corpus Christi and Austin. Those papers wanted the top comics, the top columns, and so the syndicate told Mr. Huntress, "Well, you have to pay more for the territory, which is worth more now, because we have these two papers wanting to buy that."

He didn't see it that way. By then he'd become very autocratic, and he made the decision to tell them he wouldn't do it. He'd been here so long and had such absolute authority he didn't hesitate to make decisions like that. It didn't seem to occur to him that maybe the syndicate wouldn't go along with him. It was sort of traditional in the business that you didn't take features away from a paper.

I have in my possession all the correspondence that led up to this; I'm one of the few people to know exactly what I'm talking about, and in reading the correspondence you can see this building up to a climax. One would write a letter and say "You must do it," and the other would write a letter back and say "I'm not going to do it." Then a little later on the syndicate would say, "Well, if you don't do this we're going to have to take this action." And he'd say, "Do what you want to."

You could see the executives on the *Express* side and the Huntress family didn't believe they'd ever do anything, but you can see the will hardening of the Chicago Tribune Syndicate on the other side to do it. Finally they decided to take all those away from the *Express* and *News*—about 20 comics, I'd say, plus principal columns, probably 30 all together. Dick Tracy, Little Orphan Annie, Lil Abner, comics like that. They were an integral part of the newspaper. The syndicate offered them to the *Light*. The man who handled it told me this story. I don't have this in writing, but they offered it to the publisher of the *Light* and he said, "No, it costs too much." It was about $450 a week.

The salesman said, "Why don't you ask the people in your headquarters? I'll pay for the call if you'll do it." So he persuaded Colonel Horner, the publisher of the *Light*, to pick up the telephone. Fortunately they've got somewhat cooler heads up there, and the man said immediately, "Buy, right now, sign the contract, today." Which he did.

I don't know exactly what the reaction of Huntress was. I was working here then, but I was not on the level where I talked to them; I was Sunday editor, as a matter of fact. They didn't tell us about it. There was going to be a date in the future, it was about six or eight weeks off. We'd bought other comics and could have substituted them one at a time, and drop one of the others, so there would not be the shock value. They didn't do that.

The *Light*, I later learned, expected that to happen and was prepared to put out a supplement each day and bring the comics up to date. They were astonished when they saw it coming. Every day that went by they realized that was going to be one less day they were going to have to have a recapitulation of it. They ran the comics right up to the day they stopped in the *Express*.

Then, I believe it was on a Friday afternoon, they notified those of us who handled things like that we'd have all these new comics starting Monday morning, and we had to take care of it. They didn't give us any kind of explanation of what happened to the others. For some reason or another they didn't anticipate that maybe the readers might object to that, so no one was giving any sort of explanation to the readers.

Well, when we picked up the paper on Sunday, here we've got all brand new comics and they've got all of our old comics, plus their old ones, over there. You talk about firestorms! That phone began to ring Sunday morning, and it rang all Sunday afternoon. The people getting out the Monday morning paper could barely get anything done for they didn't know what to tell them, so they didn't tell them anything.

That continued for two or three days, and finally we had some sort of lame excuse, I forget exactly what, but the damage was done. All at once circulation began to just drop. People seemed to resent that no consideration or explanation was given them, that they were supposed to just accept it and take something else, more than the actual loss of the comics. As a result, 30 days later the *Light* was first in circulation, the *Express* was second and the *News* was third. In one month's time.

It's the only thing like that has every happened in the annals of American journalism. And it was completely avoidable. I would say that it cost the stockholders of the Express Publishing Co. in excess of a half billion dollars.

The Brackenridge Estate Loses the *Express-News*

I'll tell you, they lost control of the company completely. They lost the profits they may have made during the next 15 to 20 years, the value of the newspapers diminished and they lost the TV station, which at one time could have been sold for about $350 million. Can't be sold for that today. And it was unnecessary. That was 1953, and it took us until 1975—22 years—to get the lead back in circulation.

Advertising follows circulation. Advertising went down. The second month we had a bloodbath; the department heads were called in and told to get rid of about half of their personnel, in all departments. The news staff was cut in half, the news hole was reduced. It was a terrible thing. Apparently it was something nobody could do anything about, but old Mr. Huntress had made the decision and he stuck with it. He was going to go down with the ship. Not too long after that he did stop, for his health became worse and his son took over. But it was a long hard fight getting it back.

The paper struggled along and wasn't paying dividends to stockholders. The people who owned the 27 percent were families that didn't live here and wanted to sell. There was a broker here who saw it as an opportunity. There were 4,000 shares involved, and he got it and started looking for a buyer. Tried all over the United States, but nobody wanted to buy because the papers looked like they were going under.

Then somebody told him that somebody out in West Texas, in either Abilene or San Angelo, some people named Harte-Hanks, would probably buy a newspaper like that. They called Houston Harte Sr. and he bought it over the telephone. He bought 27 percent. I wish I knew how many shares. It was sold for $4,000 a share. But it wasn't much.

After that was a period of about a year or two when for the first time the Huntress family had a minority stockholder who was on the board, had members there who knew the newspaper business, were objecting to decisions, and that sort of thing. About that time the ownership of the Express Publishing Co. stock bought the Brackenridge Estate, which was controlled by the Huntress family, which made up the board of directors. And the Brackenridge will became in doubt.

Now, this is a story that has never been told before. I have the documentation on this. There were two attorneys in town named Jesse Oppenheimer, both of them attorneys, both from an old, old family. They are cousins. One of the Oppenheimers wanted to run for the board of directors of the Robert B. Green Hospital District, now the Bexar County Hospital District. The Huntresses didn't like the other Oppenheimer, but got the two confused, so they came out and helped defeat the one that was running for the Robert B. Green board.

But he wasn't the man they thought he was. They had the wrong one. It was the cousin, Jesse H. Oppenheimer—who's a very good attorney, very bright guy, but also one who had no love for the Huntress family after that.

Jessie H. Oppenheimer began to see things he didn't think were legal in the way the Brackenridge Estate was being operated. He had a friend who happened to be attorney general of Texas, and so he asked him to investigate. The attorney general came in and investigated and his report was yes, that was true, they were doing some things. The Huntress family had to either give up the Brackenridge Estate or sell their stock in the Express Publishing Co. So they put the Brackenridge Estate stock, which I believe was 37 percent, on the market and there were some attempted sales, but nothing worked.

Finally, Mr. Harte told them he would give them $4,000 a share for it. He was the only bidder, so he bought the 37 percent which gave him control. Suddenly the Huntresses were the minority interest. Then Mr. Harte called him up and said, "I'll buy your shares, too, for the same price." So within a couple of months' time the Huntresses went from control of the company to zero.

After that was concluded in 1963, Harte-Hanks had 100 percent control. They had been very successful in operation of medium-sized newspapers and small newspapers. They put money into the company, and we began to grow. But the money was not put in that was necessary, because the *Light* was in a very strong position. They dominated advertising, they dominated circulation.

Finally in 1971, Harte-Hanks went public, became a public company, and that meant an entirely different management and left us dealing with a lot of people who were MBAs and didn't know a whole lot about the newspaper business.

So from about 1963 to the period of 1971, we had the whole Harte-Hanks family or the new managers of the Harte-Hanks—what's now the Harte-Hanks Communications—in control. They didn't invest the money they should have. When you're behind it takes more money to come up, and we did not make a great deal of progress.

Enter Rupert Murdoch

Finally they decided they would sell the company, get what they could, pay off some short-term debt. One family stockholder was complaining about the size of debt. Rupert Murdoch, an Australian with major holdings in England who was living in New York, heard about it and bought the company for about $18 million. That was Dec. 19, 1973.

That became a new era, when the scale began to be weighted in favor of the *Express-News,* because he was an operator. He had made a lifelong specialty of buying papers that were in second and third position and taking them to the first. Then he put a lot of money into it.

His instruction when he asked me to stay as head of the company was to improve the paper in any way possible to the point where it would be the best paper in Texas. People were not happy with the delivery system; improve the delivery system so every reader got the paper when and where and when he wanted it. Publicize and promote the paper and reach all the people who weren't taking the paper, show them the changes that had been made. Those were the three principles. People were always coming in and wanting to know how we did it. Well, that's the way we did it. We did those three things.

Another turning point was when the morning *Express* and the evening *News* were merged, and all of a sudden the *Express-News* had a numbers advantage and circulation over the *Light*. It was a gamble that we took. We knew the lives of afternoon papers in the United States were going to be short because of the difficulty in distribution and the pressure on people for time; afternoon paper circulation was going to diminish. Take the *Denver Post* for an example. One day it was an afternoon paper, the next day it was a morning paper.

We decided to do ours gradually and try to merge the afternoon paper into the morning paper, which we did over a period of time. There had never been but one Sunday paper, so it'd always been the *Express-News* on Sunday. Somewhere about 1955 or '56, we merged the Saturday editions together. So people were accustomed to getting Saturday and Sunday as the *Express-News,* so it wasn't too big a stretch to go from Monday to Friday.

The morning paper, the *Express*, always had the best demographics. Even when the *Light* had considerably more circulation than the *Express*, the *Express* had the things advertisers look at—income, credit cards, people who fly on airplanes, travel, own more than one home, the upper end of the market. We maintained that. We also maintained readership of people in the farms and small towns throughout the area.

When we got the numbers back it became pretty clear which was going to win. And we knew, six or seven years before the final merger with the *Light*, that there would be only one paper here, because we were climbing and increasing in advertising and readership and in profits and they were declining.

You know, I'd spent a good part of my life trying to run the *Light* out of business and worked very hard at doing it. I knew it was a matter of survival for us. I knew with the national trends. They could not exist. When it happened I was really sorry. I was sad. You hate to see a paper die, hate to see people lose their jobs. I had some regrets that we had done it, although we really had no choice.

People find this hard to believe, but I think the people who worked on the newspaper regretted the passing more than the readers did, because they missed the spirit of competition. It was a healthy thing generally speaking, sometimes it wasn't quite so healthy, because it got too intense. Everybody works harder when they have competition.

I see already that the *Express-News* will be a far better newspaper, a bigger newspaper with more resources. I don't expect people to be all that thrilled about it. They will lament that there's only one newspaper in town, only one voice. There's not any less competition, you know.

That's one of the great myths, that if you only have one paper that you don't have any more competition. The competition is not newspaper versus newspaper, newspaper versus television, newspaper versus radio. It's competition for the individual's time.

Jesse H. Oppenheimer: *A View from the Inside*

Longtime attorney Jesse H. Oppenheimer served on the predecessor board of the Bexar County Hospital District.

I was born and raised here, as were both of my parents; my father was raised on the corner of Pecan and Jefferson and my mother was in a home known as the Halff House, still located on HemisFair Plaza. I've always had a strong community involvement, including in events that led up to the change in ownership of the Express Publishing Co.

It all started in the late 1950s and early '60s when I was appointed by Bexar County Commissioners Court to the board of what was then called the Robert B. Green Hospital, now the Bexar County Hospital District. While I served, the question of a medical school for this area arose. Due to the strenuous efforts of some very good citizens, it was finally determined that if a satisfactory site could be selected, a medical school would be located in San Antonio.

All medical schools are attached to what is called a "teaching hospital." It was obvious at the time that the Robert B. Green was not large enough or adequate to be that teaching hospital. All medical schools that have teaching hospitals rely to a great extent on charity cases, public cases, in order to teach students, interns and residents, and you have to have a very large population in a hospital in order to afford this.

At that time, the board of the Green was unanimous that the school and its related facilities be in the downtown area adjacent to the Robert B. Green. At the time, Winston Martin was head of Urban Renewal, and I knew his input would be valuable. We were told that land could be obtained through urban renewal for the medical school and all its supporting facilities. There was a large group of downtown merchants, headed principally by Pat Zachry, who also believed strongly that the facility should be downtown. At one meeting I witnessed, he raised a million dollars in pledges in about an hour in order to buy more land that was needed in excess of what Urban Renewal could supply.

Looking at the other side of the coin, the group of developers headed by Edgar von Scheel and McCreless and others had purchased for a fairly nominal amount quite a few hundred acres where the medical school is now situated. We called it the "Country Club location," because Oak Hills Country Club was out there. At the same time another force militated that with the new Methodist Hospital you had an existing suburban hospital located out there. So you had a combination of the developers and supporters of Methodist Hospital who wanted to build the medical school and related facilities out where it's presently located.

The developers did a very clever thing done often by developers. When they buy some land, they often donate certain portions for a school or a church. That sort of thing makes their land more valuable and also complies with the public needs. This was what was done pretty much with the medical center. If you can visualize a doughnut, the developers transferred the hole in the doughnut—I think it was around 200 acres—to the San Antonio Medical Foundation. And of course they retained the doughnut, the bulk of the land out there, which they bought by the acre but later could sell by the square foot.

They formed a very fine group of people to head this foundation. Jim Hollers, a political dentist, became very large in that group, later head of it. Their function was to see that they prevailed on having the medical school and other public facilities placed on that 200 acres. This would of course tremendously enhance the value of the remaining land, which has been highly successful as a real estate development.

Attorney Jesse H. Oppenheimer.

So we had this struggle going on between the board of the Green or the hospital district and these down-town-oriented people against the developers and the key people with the Methodist Hospital. And of course we weren't getting paid anything; we considered ourselves working as volunteers for the public. Although we did our best, I don't imagine we did it 24 hours a day.

They would send in committees and commissions to make studies of the relative merits of the two locations, and we would see Jim Hollers and others entertaining these people on various occasions.

Merton Minter was one of the outstanding internists in San Antonio, and the guru for general practitioners out at the Methodist Hospital. For some reason or other, and I don't know just how it happened, he became extremely interested in having the medical school out where it's presently located.

He also, and this was the key, was on the board of regents of the University of Texas. At this time the Methodist was just a rural hospital, outlying hospital, to service the needs of the northern part of San Antonio. Merton Minter's wife was the sister of Frank Huntress Jr., who ran the Express Publishing Co.

Through that connection, I believe, the Express Publishing Co. became deeply involved and aggressively involved in seeing to it that the medical school and its supporting facilities and the new county hospital were built out at what we considered the "country club site," or the developers' location. This was in the very late '50s and early '60s.

At that time there was a columnist on the *News* front page, left side, by the name of Paul Thompson. The trustees of the Bexar County Hospital District were unanimously in favor of the downtown location. They had no motivation, no monetary motivation, except what they thought was good for the community, in putting the charity hospital closer to the charity cases, which were mainly on the West Side of San Antonio. And Paul Thompson began running column after column after column about the Robert B. Green board, in many instances exaggerations, to say the least, and lies, to say the most.

Slowly, as our terms expired, we were replaced on that board by people sympathetic with the North Side site. We used to get a kick out of Paul Thompson—he called the other eight a "clique." The one person he treated like he was the majority, he always called the eight to one; I forget whether the board was seven or whether it was nine.

At that point I became rather enraged. I'm a cause person anyway, and go off on tangents when I see some injustice. I knew that the Express Publishing Co. control rested with the Brackenridge Estate. I also knew the Brackenridge Estate had done little or nothing for charity in our community. It was set up as a charitable trust for educational purposes, and been attacked back in the '20s or the '30s. It was owned 28 percent by the Huntresses personally, 33 1/3 percent by the Brackenridge Charitable Trust, and the balance by who we used to refer to as the Grice heirs, who lived in Chicago. They had received little or no dividends and little or no recognition of their ownership because they were minority shareholders, and they were trying to sell their stock.

The Huntresses along with Leroy Denman and a man by the name of McDaniels, who worked with the Huntresses, and two Huntresses were the trustees of the Brackenridge Trust. By the ownership of one-third of the trust and their ability to vote that stock and the 28 percent that they owned individually, they were able to control the corporation. I have in my possession many of the minutes of their meetings and also many of their financial statements over the years.

George Brackenridge died around 1919. His will was probated in 1920 or 1921. During that entire period, little or nothing had been given to charity, and the Huntresses along with their supporters, including McDaniels and Denman, were able to vote the stock and make themselves directors of the corporation and to elect themselves officers.

So here we had a three-tiered layer cake of them as trustees of a charitable trust electing themselves directors of the corporation, electing themselves as officers and doing little or nothing for charity according to Mr. Brackenridge's wishes. As a matter of fact, their first tax exemption from the Internal Revenue Service was not obtained until 1962. They didn't even have tax exemption.

The Huntresses knew that anything the corporation did in the way of expansion and growth would enhance and improve the value of their interest, so they voted their 28 percent plus the 33 1/3 percent interest toward acquisition of radio stations, television stations and air service to the Valley, plowing back the earnings of the Express Publishing Co. into these acquisitions, which in turn plowed Mr. Brackenridge's funds, as well. They had not made any substantial contributions, only token amounts at the time that I became aware of it in 1961 and 1962.

One of my closest friends was B. F. Pittman, who was in investment banking. The Grice heirs had come to him and said they wanted to sell their stock. He got hold of Houston Harte Sr., who had the San Angelo *Times* and the *Caller* down in Corpus Christi, and asked if he wanted to buy their stock. Mr. Harte said, yes, he did, and he bought the stock at $4,000 per share. So now Harte-Hanks owned the Grice heirs' interest in the *Express*, but it was a minority interest.

I went up and looked into their positions with the company and got information from Ben Pittman, who had it from the Grice heirs. I determined they were using this charitable trust for their own purposes. I wrote a memorandum, about 20 pages, on their conflict of interest and how they had to either sell the Express Publishing Co. stock or had to resign as trustees. I sent it to Will Wilson, who was the Texas attorney general and the only person charged by law with enforcement of charitable trusts. He agreed that he would do something about it. In fact, they drafted a petition asking them to resign.

So Harte offered them $10,000 a share for the Brackenridge Trust stock. They sold him their 28 percent at $10,000 dollars a share, and he bought it. So at that point Harte-Hanks became 100 percent owners of the Express Publishing Co.

Index